PERIPHERAL VISIONS FOR WRITING CENTERS

PERIPHERAL VISIONS FOR WRITING CENTERS

JACKIE GRUTSCH McKINNEY

UTAH STATE UNIVERSITY PRESS
Logan

© 2013 by the University Press of Colorado
Published by Utah State University Press
An imprint of University Press of Colorado
5589 Arapahoe Avenue, Suite 206C
Boulder, Colorado 80303

 The University Press of Colorado is a proud member of
The Association of American University Presses.

The University Press of Colorado is a cooperative publishing enterprise supported, in part, by
Adams State University, Colorado State University, Fort Lewis College, Metropolitan State University
of Denver, Regis University, University of Colorado, University of Northern Colorado, Utah State
University, and Western State Colorado University.

ISBN: 978-0-87421-916-6 (e-book)
ISBN: 978-0-87421-915-9 (paper)

Library of Congress Cataloging-in-Publication Data
Grutsch McKinney, Jackie.
  Peripheral visions for writing centers / Jackie Grutsch McKinney.
     pages cm
  Includes bibliographical references and index.
  ISBN 978-0-87421-915-9 (pbk.) — ISBN 978-0-87421-916-6 (e-book)
1. Writing centers. 2. English language—Rhetoric—Study and teaching. 3. Report writing—Study
and teaching (Higher) I. Title.
  PE1404.G78 2013
  808'.042071—dc23
                              2012050038

An earlier version of "Chapter Three: Writing Centers Are Cozy" was published as "Leaving Home
Sweet Home: Towards Critical Readings of Writing Center Spaces" in *The Writing Center Journal* 25, no.
2 (2005): 6–20. A research grant from the International Writing Center Association helped support
the survey project ("Beyond Tutoring") conducted with Rebecca Jackson and cited in Chapter 4.

For Todd, Bennett, and Spencer, of course. My whole heart.

CONTENTS

ACKNOWLEDGMENTS

I'd be remiss not to acknowledge all of the support and encouragement that helped turn a blurry vision into the book you now read.

First of all, I acknowledge my deep gratitude for the administrators, tutors, and writers who I've come to know working in three different writing centers over the last two decades. These centers have been places of chaos and respite, inspiration and routine, collaboration and conflict—indeed, spaces of radical possibility, to borrow bell hooks's phrase.

From my very first email to Utah State University Press, editor Michael Spooner has been generous with praise, encouragement, and advice. Michael was more than patient with my first-time author questions and worries. In addition, Laura Furney and her team at University Press of Colorado were wonderful to work with and made the production process painless. The anonymous reviewers of my manuscript were likewise generous with their enthusiasm for the project and their detailed, spot-on revision suggestions. Thank you.

Though many fields are permeated with a cutthroat, competitive ethos, writing center studies, luckily, is usually not. I'm so grateful for the encouragement of many writing center scholars I admire. Clint Gardner's and Neal Lerner's early praise for "Leaving Home Sweet Home" made me believe I was onto something. Patron Saint of Writing Centers Mickey Harris's general faith in my work gave me buoyancy: one of her encouraging emails is printed and taped in my office at eye-level, a virtual pep talk for difficult days. Attending the 2008 IWCA Summer Institute to learn from leaders Brad Hughes, Lisa Ede, Neal Lerner, Nancy Grimm, Paula Gillespie, among others was the best professional experience I've ever had and in more ways than one pushed me to follow through with this project.

I'm thankful for my mentors and teachers—classroom and otherwise—who helped me improve as a scholar, critic, writer, and human over the years, especially Elizabeth Chiseri-Strater, Hepsie Roskelly, Nancy Myers, Rebecca Jackson, and Kris Fleckenstein. I'm equally thankful for my grad student colleagues who continue to exchange ideas, drafts, successes, and tales of woe with me.

Over the last nine years, I've been lucky to have the warm support of my friends and colleagues in the English Department at Ball State

University. I stayed sane with help of *the ladies*, especially Debbie Mix and Jill Christman, who can talk me up and talk me down (from the edge) better than any friends I've ever had. I'm also grateful for the university's research support and especially for the research assistants who have helped with this project—Claire Luktewitte, Erin Banks-Kirkham, and Ashley Ellison Murphy.

My sweet little boys, Bennett and Spencer, deserve thanks for sharing me with this project for the last couple of years. Mama owes you ice cream. With sprinkles.

Finally, it is not an exaggeration to say the book would not exist without Todd McKinney. My partner and best friend, Todd literally and figuratively wheeled me back in front of my writing desk, faithfully read pages and pages of drafts, and allowed me to interrupt him for impromptu writing conferences over and over again. Alabadoo.

"Every story one chooses to tell is a kind of censorship: it prevents the telling of other tales."

—Salman Rushdie (2000), *Shame*

1

INTRODUCTION
Cognitive Dissonance

Are we afraid that no one will do it if we talk about the real deal?
—Beth Boquet (2002), *Noise from the Writing Center*

A typical day for a writing center director might include any of the following:

- Writing job ads, posting job ads, answering questions about job ads, asking for references for applicants, interviewing applicants, hiring applicants
- Preparing for staff meetings, discussing tutoring needs with staff, finding guest speakers
- Training tutors, observing tutors, giving tutors suggestions for improving practices, locating readings for tutors, distributing copies to tutors, listening to tutors' self-assessment and their suggestions for improving the writing center
- Answering questions about commas or APA or *kairos* while walking past a tutoring session, answering questions about commas or APA or *kairos* while getting mail in faculty mailroom or at retirement dinners or on airplanes
- Writing or proofing copy for writing center advertisements, giving an interview to the school paper on the usefulness of a writing center
- Writing conference proposals or presentations, drafting articles, tracking down out-of-print books from interlibrary loan
- Coaching tutors or graduate students in writing proposals, articles, theses, dissertations, or job letters
- Meeting with student groups and faculty who want to know how the writing center can help them, meeting with student groups and faculty who want to know all the "secrets" to being good writers in an hour or less
- Writing memos articulating needs for more space, better equipment, more tutoring bodies; writing reports on utilization of space, equipment, and tutoring bodies
- Scheduling tutors, rescheduling tutors, taking calls from sick and delayed tutors, finding replacements, telling students their tutor is late or their tutor is not coming
- Tutoring student writers from all levels on all sorts of projects, consciously hoping to model "good tutoring practices" to others in the room

- Answering emails and phone calls from disappointed students who want more appointments, answering emails and phone calls from faculty members who want miracles
- Meetings: all kinds
- Delegating: as much as possible
- Reading latest (or thereabout) issues of the *Writing Center Journal*, the *Writing Lab Newsletter*, *Praxis*, *Writing Program Administrator*, *College Composition and Communication*, *College English*, and other related publications
- Maintaining careful records; maintaining the writing center website, blog, Twitter, and Facebook
- Ordering supplies, books, equipment, furniture, pens, bookmarks
- Meeting with students or faculty who are researching student writers in the writing center, discussing ethical research practices, methodologies, and historical approaches to writing center research
- Troubleshooting computer problems, software programs, network problems
- Responding to posts from other writing center professionals on WCENTER
- Running for a regional writing center association board, voting in board elections, hosting regional or national writing center conferences, packing up for travel to a city-wide, mini-regional, regional, national, or international meeting with other writing center professionals
- Cleaning tables, chairs, keyboards; tidying up resources and desk drawers
- Meeting with university assessment and accreditation committees to negotiate assessment plans
- Talking with tutors and students about their weekends, classes, money and relationship problems, and favorite YouTube videos
- Worrying about what is not getting done, what is not getting done well, or what the university's financial crisis might mean for the students, tutors, and you

Since many writing center directors are also faculty, days may also be full of teaching tasks: reading, lesson planning, syllabus writing, conferences, going to class, grading, responding to emails, as well as faculty meetings and committee work. For some faculty writing center directors, doing research is essential for keeping a job and being promoted, so days are also full of drafting proposals, communicating with co-authors, writing, researching, and revising. Since it is not uncommon for a writing center director to maintain a research agenda in a different subfield (say, Early Modern English or Basic Writing), some must keep current in two areas of study: writing center studies and their research area.

Writing center tutors have equally complex lives. As tutors, they have many of the responsibilities that directors do, in addition to other tasks. They must get to work, clock in, answer phone calls and emails, work with students in tutoring sessions, work with students who walk in with any number of questions, work with faculty with any number of questions, complete records or paperwork, troubleshoot computer and software problems, prepare for and attend staff meetings, work on writing center training materials or publications, complete peer or self-assessments, track down obscure rules for manuscript guidelines in Chicago style or gerunds or resumé formatting, provide cultural insider insights on American academic expectations, negotiate highly charged sessions or, alternatively, apathetic students, and teach students how to research and revise. Tutors are often students as well. They may be undergraduates carrying eighteen-credit hours each term with classes all over campus or they might be graduate students with intense reading, writing, and research workloads.

In addition, all directors and tutors are immersed in a workplace with colleagues, histories, and expectations, all of which may be easy or difficult to manage depending on their contexts. And, as all writing center directors and tutors are also humans, days are permeated with personal and familial relationships, responsibilities, and the daily minutia of keeping ourselves and maybe others fed, well, clean, and rested.

Yet, if I'm invited to talk about what happens in a writing center or what I do as a writing center director, I don't typically talk about much of this. I say something about how a writing center is a place for all students to get feedback on their writing and how I supervise the tutors. To be sure, when asked what I do, no one really wants to hear a laundry list like the one above. And, of course, writing center directors and tutors do not necessarily have it any easier or harder than others in terms of the work they do. However, I've started to listen to how I talk about the work of the writing center, and I'm curious how I select from this list of what to say. What can be understood from that rhetorical choice?

The main argument of this book is that writing center work is complex, but the storying of writing center work is not. By and large, the way that writing center scholars, practitioners, and outsiders talk about writing center work fits into a relatively familiar pattern, similar to mine above. In the following chapters, I examine that familiar pattern. I call it the writing center grand narrative, which goes something like this: *writing centers are comfortable, iconoclastic places where all students go to get one-to-one tutoring on their writing.* Like any grand narrative, there is some truth in this description of writing center work. Throughout this book,

I am not concerned with arguing that this narrative is patently untrue. It's not. Instead, I am making the case for considering two things. First, by telling this story, what story am I not allowing? What story am I censoring, to use Salman Rushdie's words from the epigraph? Second, by telling this story, what do I gain and what do I lose?

This book, then, addresses the cognitive dissonance between the work we do and the work we talk about. There are moments when I get five minutes, fifty minutes, or maybe even more to spin whatever story I would like about our writing center, and up until lately, I have to admit, I have not told my writing center story with much foresight or much afterthought. I have borrowed the story from the discipline; this story is committed to my unconscious memory. Like how a rosary bead compels one to a particular prayer, on an occasion for talking about writing centers, I return to the same story. Aside from getting this off my chest, none of this would be particularly important to air publicly, no less in book-length form, except for the fact that I am not the only one using this narrative, and for those of us who use it, I think the telling has become so naturalized, so transparent, that we no longer recognize our tellings and retellings as one of many possible representations. Instead, telling the familiar writing center story is just what we do.

Muriel Harris has written that there is no easy way to communicate to others in our institutions about the work we do. She writes, "The types of work accomplished in writing center tutorials are so complex and varied—and individualized—that we have not yet been able to come up with sound bytes that illuminate what we do" (Harris 2007, 75). And though I think she is right that it is too difficult to condense all that we do into a few sentences—certainly items get lost in the condensation—I do think the grand narrative is the way many of us have tacitly agreed to talk about our work and that outsiders do get a general, legible picture of writing center work from what we say.

Furthermore, telling the writing center grand narrative story makes me feel like I belong, although not locally. I do not feel more connected to those in front of me when I tell these stories; instead I feel more connected to those in writing center studies. Though in *Facing the Center* Harry Denny says the writing center community doesn't "have a code or widely agreed consensus about performativity" thus "nearly anyone can claim our identity" (Denny 2010, 149), I disagree. I think the story we keep about our work is one of our membership badges; we can discern outsiders by those who stray from the narrative. Like any other community, those in the writing center profession share some common beliefs, rituals, and lore and learn/teach others how to shape these experiences into words—members learn "rhetorical habits," in Kris Fleckenstein's (2010) terms. Knowing these habits and making them mine make me feel like I belong—all the more so if I can talk about my telling among other insiders who will validate me, laugh with me, or commiserate with me.

I do think, as I illustrate throughout, that the story is both beneficial and constraining to writing center studies. Having a grand narrative has united us, given us a "purity of purpose," as Terrance Riley (1994) asserts. Yet, the story has worked in less positive ways—like all stories have the potential to do—by changing the ways we see. It has given us a frame for seeing and evaluating writing center work. If writing centers are *comfortable, iconoclastic places where all students go to get one-to-one tutoring on their writing*, then certain activities take center stage, certain activities are legible as writing center work and others are not. Consequently, this affects job training: those entering the profession may not be prepared for the work they will be asked to do. Michael Pemberton explains, "On one particularly frustrating day, while wrestling with a writing center schedule that seemed to change every five minutes and fielding calls from faculty who wanted me to give class presentations in ten minutes, it suddenly struck me that my graduate school training and coursework had completely failed to prepare me for the parts of my job that routinely demanded the most time and energy" (Pemberton 2011, 256). I believe that because we are preoccupied by the writing center grand narrative, we routinely do not prepare future administrators for actual writing center work.

The writing center grand narrative also shapes others' views about what is writing center work. A brief anecdote might illustrate this point. During my first month on the job as a writing center director in 2003, I complained to the writing program director that the computers in the writing center were ancient and mostly unusable. The writing program director agreed and went to the department chair to ask for replacements. As I waited outside the office (in retrospect, I have no idea why I was not invited in), I hear the writing program director make the case, and I hear the chair respond: "I'm sorry, but it's not a computer lab. You know?" The chair's internalization of the writing center story—what a writing center does and thus does not do—did not include computers and, as a result, that first semester we were stuck with our ancient and unusable equipment.

The effect of the writing center grand narrative can be a sort of collective tunnel vision. The story has focused our attention so narrowly that we already no longer see the range and variety of activities that make up writing center work or the potential ways in which writing center work could evolve. Thus, the title of the book reveals its aim: peripheral vision. I would like us, myself especially, to be more conscious of the formulaic ways we story writing center work because the stories give us frames, or what Kris Fleckenstein (2010) calls "visual habits," for interpretation. In *The Everyday Writing Center*, Geller et al. note that writing center professionals are often too busy (with the sorts of tasks listed at the beginning of this chapter) to notice the everyday ways in which our writing centers are already communities of practice. They assert "the most interesting moments of our workday might have not demanded our attention at all" (Geller et al. 2007, 5). We've been conditioned not to notice these everyday moments by the interlinked rhetorical and visual habits the writing center grand narrative provides. To come to peripheral visions, we need to become aware of the narrowness of the writing center grand narrative and the tunnel vision that it enables. By doing so, we can complicate the writing center narrative in ways that include what now lies at the periphery of our work.

CHAPTER OVERVIEW

If the writing center grand narrative is a cloth woven from various strands and strings to appear as a whole, in each of the chapters that follow, I pull at one strand at a time, not to dismantle it entirely but to show how easily it unravels under pressure. Each chapter takes a small piece of the grand narrative (*writing centers are comfortable, iconoclastic places where all students go to get one-to-one tutoring on their writing*) under consideration in order to discuss how piece by piece the entire narrative is merely a representation and simultaneously a misrepresentation of writing center work. The first chapter outlines the theoretical assumptions the book relies on. There, I connect the dots between stories and vision using ideas and scholarship from within composition and writing center studies, as well as from outside of these academic areas.

After establishing the theoretical frame for my argument, I take the grand narrative apart in three chapters, each digging deeper into our most naturalized and cherished common-sense assumptions about writing center work. I imagine a reader who might get increasingly uncomfortable as he or she continues through these chapters. Yet, at the same time, although uncomfortable, that same reader might hear the collected peripheral stories of writing center work and finally be able to point to his or her own cognitive dissonance between what is said and what is enacted, what marks belonging and what does not.

In the second chapter, a revision of an article published in *Writing Center Journal* originally titled "Leaving Home Sweet Home" (Grutsch McKinney 2005), I tackle the idea that writing centers are or should be comfortable spaces. Though often described in that way—as cozy, homey, friendly, safe, and comfortable—I think of these descriptions as stories. I review some of these depictions and make the case that (1) the readings of spaces ought to consider multiple interpretations (the centers are not cozy simply if we insist they are); (2) the ideal of a cozy center might not be universally held; and (3) telling the story of our centers as cozy spaces does less to describe the lived, material realities and does more to reveal our loyalties to the writing center grand narrative. We story the physical spaces of our centers in particular ways to show our allegiance and our belonging to the writing center community.

After drafting the first version of that article, I began to wonder if there were other stories writing center professionals told one another and outsiders that painted writing center work in a particular (positive) light but did not seem to account for the whole picture of lived, material realities of writing center work. It was a small step from thinking about how writing center spaces are represented as alternative to mainstream academe to my noticing how writing center professionals and writing center scholarship is also represented as different, non-traditional, or iconoclastic. So, the third chapter confronts the idea of the writing center as a non-traditional, iconoclastic part of academic life. From very early on in writing center scholarship, scholars have insisted that writing centers should and do operate outside the mainstream of academe probably stemming from the physical placement outside of the classroom structure. This has persisted—for example, a recent collection on writing centers, *Marginal Words, Marginal Work?*, takes on this continued marginality (Macauley and Mauriello 2007a). Though some have asserted that an outsider status serves writing centers—Terrance Riley (1994) calls writing center workers "happy amateurs," for example—the narrative of writing center professionals and research as iconoclastic does not account for how writing center professionals suffer from this categorization in institutional status, graduate training, promotion, and the like.

After pushing and pulling at the naturalized ideas that writing centers are cozy and maverick spaces, I go to the heart of the writing center grand narrative by interrogating the idea that one-to-one tutoring for all students is or should be the primary work of writing centers. I begin by showing how this idea has been propagated in writing center discourse to such a degree that one-to-one tutoring, especially a particular way of tutoring, is seen as the defining quality of writing centers. A writing center would cease to be a writing center without one-to-one tutoring, wouldn't it? To counter this perception, I pursue three alternate veins. First, I trace evidence of other, non-tutoring work in writing centers throughout the decades of writing center scholarship. Throughout the history of writing center work, there have been different goals for what a writing center might do and different methods for approaching these goals. Though the grand narrative assumes the centrality of tutoring, other methods have always been in play. Second, I point to research that counters the perception that tutoring is (or works) for all students. Finally, I discuss evidence from more recent primary research of writing center work to show that in contemporary writing centers, despite the ways we story our work, writing center work exceeds appointment-based individualized instruction.

In the conclusion, I address how the writing center grand narrative functions as a part of the discourse community of writing center professionals. As such, every time writing center professionals have an opportunity to tell a writing center story, we have the opportunity to (re)invent writing center work. Though rewriting community narratives is difficult, I point to theories of how individuals and organizations can change stories to change vision.

As someone whose heart and academic home has been in the writing center community for the better part of the last decade, I am aware that years of struggle have brought us to the point where we are today. The writing center grand narrative has been hard won, where it has been won. Those involved in writing centers over the decades have had to articulate week after week, semester after semester, year after year what a writing center is, what it isn't, what it does, and what it doesn't. For this reason, some readers might regard a project that aims to complicate the story of writing centers that insiders are finally getting outsiders to digest as misguided, backward, or even blasphemous. Some might suggest that having a shared story that articulates our "purity of purpose" is crucial; I tend to agree that writing centers would not have expanded the way they have in the last few decades if the work of writing centers were not legible.

The problem, however, is that when we repeatedly tell outsiders that writing centers do x or writing centers are x, they expect x. They assess x. They fund x. And if x is an explanation, a story, meant to make the work understandable to outsiders but really only the beginning of what writing centers are, do, did, or could do, we might find ourselves having trouble getting recognized or getting funding for y or z. Moreover, those most involved in writing center work—writing center professionals—have internalized and passed down the writing center grand narrative, even if it only narrowly describes their work. Once internalized, the narrative narrows the gaze of writing center practitioners and scholars, shaping their research and practice. My work in the chapters that follow shines light on those other representations of writing center work that the grand narrative fails to account for.

2
STORY VISION

Before considering how writing center narratives shape writing center identities and work, I want to lay out my theoretical approach. Some readers may be familiar with narrative theory, perhaps in how it was traditionally used in literary analysis with texts that are overtly narratives, but might be less familiar with how it is used with texts that are not consciously "stories." However, since the mid-twentieth century, the study of narratives has become important in many disciplines. Scholars in literature, certainly, but also in linguistics, anthropology, psychoanalysis, and sociology have found the study of narratives, or narratology, a worthwhile way to study culture. The change in perception of narratives was from one in which narratives were "devices for structuring or decorating extraordinary texts" to seeing narratives as "fundamentally social and cognitive tools" (Eubanks 2004, 33). This is a departure from earlier studies of poetics or narrative that focused exclusively on literary texts. Philip Eubanks notes the "shift in perspective" in narrative studies has "opened productive avenues for the study of everyday texts" (33). To study everyday texts—such as articles, reports, conversations, or student papers—Eubanks says "one of the main tasks . . . is to document and analyze tacit narratives—narratives that legitimate, direct, and constrain discourse and practices in institutional and professional settings" (36).

Catherine Penner explains that many early theorists working in narrative theory searched for the grammar of narrative—the ways in which all stories might be "particular manifestations of shared structural systems" (Penner 1998, 195). More recently, however, this focus has shifted and "much current narrative theory focuses on the discourse of stories—the ways in which their tellers enact culture in communicating with readers or listeners" (196). The result, Penner says, is that "narratology effectively banished from narrative criticism any sense of stories as transparent vehicles for discernible realities or unproblematic visions of individually animated minds creating their own meaning" (195). In other words, stories are not seen as simple reports of events or facts, nor are they seen as formed in the minds of individual writers apart from or unaffected by culture, material conditions, or context.

The term I used throughout the introduction, "grand narrative," came to the forefront as this shift in narrative study occurred. The idea, also used interchangeably with the terms *master narrative* or *metanarrative*, is attributed to Jean-Francois Lyotard and is a way to describe powerful yet often invisible narratives that work to explain how disparate pieces fit into a cohesive whole. Eubanks says postmodernism asks us to be attuned to these grand narratives that are "stories that pervade, shape, and, it is often asserted, delude cultures" (Eubanks 2004, 35). The idea is so central to postmodernism, in fact, that Lyotard asserts, "I define postmodern as incredulity toward metanarratives" (Lyotard 1984, xxiv).

In James Berlin's words, grand narratives are "the stories we tell about our experiences that attempt to account for all features of it" (Berlin 1992, 19). Instead of believing that the grand narrative is the only narrative, postmodern critics "look for what is left out, what exists on the unspoken margins of culture" (20). Berlin says this is "history from the bottom up, telling the stories of the people and events normally excluded from totalizing accounts" (20). Once we hear those stories, once we cast doubt on the adequacy of the grand narrative, we can come to see that "no claims can be offered as absolute, timeless truths since all are historically specific, arising in response to the conditions of a particular time and place" (23).

I see the writing center grand narrative functioning similarly. It is a story that pulls together certain disparate events, ideas, and actions in order to tell a coherent or totalizing story about writing centers. And the story, once in motion, excludes other ideas about writing centers that do not fit with the established writing center story. It is also so absolutely "normal," so tacit, that it functions invisibly. It seems not to be a story, a representation, but more a definition, a fact, a truth. For this reason, I'm calling the story a grand narrative and treating it as such in my analysis.

Yet, some might wonder how *writing centers are comfortable, iconoclastic places where all students go to get one-to-one tutoring on their writing* is a narrative at all, let alone a grand narrative. They might wonder, how is it a story? Though it could be called a definition, a vision, an articulation, I use "story" to draw attention to the fact that it is constructed; telling a story is motivated by what I want to highlight and what I do not. In that way, what I say is certainly rhetorical, yet the messages take a distinctly narrative form. Stories paint pictures with characters, conflict, plot twists, settings, and resolutions. Further, I like that the word "story" implies an account that may have one foot in fiction and one foot in nonfiction. I certainly think what I am calling the "writing center grand narrative" is both true and untrue in its correspondence to some sort of reality; talking about this as a narrative is a way to explain how that can be. Since I am especially interested in talking about the "people and events normally excluded," that is, those stories on the periphery, framing my discussion as narrative critique gives me language for this undertaking.

NARRATIVE STUDY IN COMPOSITION

Of course, many scholars in composition studies have used narrative theory to problematize dominant narratives that abound within the discipline. For example, in "History in the Spaces Left: African American Presence and Narratives of Composition Studies," Jacqueline Jones Royster and Jean Williams take to task historical narratives of composition that flatten out in complexity upon retelling resulting in exclusionary "officialized" narratives, that "set the agenda for how and whether other narratives can operate with consequence, and they also set the measures of universality—that is, the terms by which we assign generality, validity, reliability, credibility, significance, authority, and so forth" (Royster and Williams 1999, 580). They note that one of the troubling narratives in composition studies, propagated by Mina Shaughnessy (1977), is that there were few students of color in colleges and universities (and thus in composition classrooms) until open admissions in the 1960s. Royster and Williams remind readers that there were land-grant institutions for African Americans as early as the 1890s as well as other opportunities for higher education for people of color well before the 1960s. Using this as just one example, the authors want to see "a systematic commitment to resist the primacy of 'officialized' narratives" (Royster and Williams 1999, 582). Royster and Williams ask for composition scholars to "pay more attention to the shadows and to how unnoticed dimensions of composition history might interact with officialized narratives to tell a reconfigured, more fully textured story" (581).

Another example is *The Activist WPA* by Linda Adler-Kassner, who discusses the problem of the national story of student writing—that students can't write and teachers don't teach the right stuff—and its effect on the work of writing teachers and writing program administrators. She writes to encourage other stories to challenge the dominant narrative: "What doesn't come up as often in news media or in conversation are stories suggesting something else—that everyone can write; that students are astoundingly knowledgeable about composing in contexts that some teachers know relatively little about; that schools are being put in virtually untenable situations with regard to literacy instruction; or that it might be worth questioning the criteria by which 'quality' is being determined" (Adler-Kassner 2008, 1). Her work comes from a "desire to work from different stories—in fact to change the dominant story about the work of writing instruction" (2).

In addition, composition scholars have pointed out grand narratives in composition scholarship. Beth Daniell writes about what she dubs the two grand narratives in composition scholarship in "Narratives of Literacy: Connection Composition to Culture." She states that "Lyotard argues that in the modern age knowledge is justified, or legitimated, through narrative. The legitimacy of an idea, a work, or a proposal depends, in other words, on its contribution to one of two grand narratives" (Daniell 1999, 393). The narratives used in composition studies, Daniell suggests, are teachers as the heroes of knowledge or teachers as the heroes of liberty. In these, teachers are cast into the role as savior to their charges. Daniell warns, however, "The point is that we must all be careful of literacy narratives that make us feel good" (401). Similarly, in "Subverting the Academic Master Plot" Lynn Bloom (1997) suggests that scholarship in composition studies has two basic master plots: the miracle cure and the dramatic change plots. Again, in both of these stories, the teacher overcomes great obstacles to save the class or to educate the seemingly uneducable. Both Daniell and Bloom thus articulate an understanding of how individual practitioners weave their tale to conform to particular cultural expectations of how to tell a "composition story." The deconstruction of these sorts of tales is also taken up in Rich Haswell and Min-Zhan Lu's (2007) *Comp Tales* and Joseph Trimmer's (1997) collection *Narration as Knowledge.*

Likewise, writing center scholars have also used narrative to make arguments and to deconstruct existing ones. In many cases, as is the case for *Stories from the Center*, writing center scholars consciously construct narratives about writing center work to tell their writing center story. Editors Lynn Craigue Briggs and Meg Woolbright make their edited collection *Stories from the Center* a space for sharing writing center stories because "so many publications about writing centers seemed to sweep away complexity, to reduce tutoring/consulting/responding to a set of seven steps or five categories, to streamline policy and procedures, and to offer simple 'solutions' to 'problems'" (Briggs and Woolbright 2000, x). They categorize the narratives in the collection as "academic narratives" because they twist story and theory together as opposed to "studies" or "study-like discourse" that the editors want to resist (xi). Academic narrative, they assert, is "more humanistic, more humane, more 'fun' . . . rigorous and truthful" (xvi).

In other places, like in Melissa Nicolas's "Why There Is No Happily Ever After," writing center scholars question writing center narratives. Nicolas spins the writing center origin story as a fable in order to theorize about the writing center's place in the institution and to question the coding of writing, of writing centers, and writing center work as feminine. That is, she consciously wants us to pay attention to the narrative aspect of writing center lore. I agree with her assertion that "as we transition into the next generation [of writing center work], it is important to reflect on the stories we have collected in our lore and scholarship because much of what happens in writing centers' second generation will be in response to the foundation that has been laid during the past two-and-a-half decades" (Nicolas 2007, 4).

In a similar vein, in the opening to *Facing the Center*, Harry Denny consciously plays with the notion of storytelling. He begins the book by writing, "I could tell a tale of swagger and pride" (Denny 2010, 1). Yet, in the very next paragraph, Denny cautions us, "Just as easily, I could reflect on those very same writing centers and tell another tale of ongoing struggle to train the staff" (1). Instead of telling either of those stories (or in addition to those two stories), Denny writes, "I want to tell another tale, a set of tales in fact, rooted in a phenomenon that cuts across writing centers, that resists easy answers and offers up tough questions, that invites problem-posing and believing and doubting" (2). Thus, Denny asks us to remember that storytelling is not a reporting of facts, that stories are motivated by authorial intentions and perspectives—even in academic writing. We always choose what story to tell and which to leave untold, consciously or not.

Moreover, more and more writing center scholarship is emerging that doesn't just use narrative as a rhetorical strategy but takes the adequacy of common writing center narratives under consideration. For example, in 2008 the *Writing Center Journal* devoted an entire issue to articles that interrogated writing center stories. Here, in "Attending to the Conceptual Change Potential of Writing Center Narratives," Nancy Grimm argues that how we tell stories about writing center work has a moral dimension. She argues that "we can tutor literacy and represent the work of a writing center with attention to the structural frames of historical privileges and unequal social relationships rather than reduce literacy to an individual skill" (Grimm 2008, 7), if we better examine our motives, cultural norms, and the contexts of our stories. Also in this issue, Rebecca Jackson (2008) tells a "counterstory" of one student who did not and would not fit into the characterization afforded to her in writing center narratives. These articles, along with ones by Meg Carroll (2008) and Kathryn Valentine (2008), are fine examples of how writing center scholars have used narrative theory to push at the boundaries of writing center work.

Importantly, Phillip Gardner and William Ramsey have previously pointed to a writing center grand narrative in "The Polyvalent Mission of Writing Centers." Gardner and Ramsey trace a antagonistic, contrarian strain in writing center scholarship and warn of its consequences for writing center work. In brief, they find a writing center grand narrative of resistance creates a false binary of vision for practitioners. We come to believe we can take one of two paths. Gardner and Ramsey's supposition that "whatever narrative we write about our professional selves limits us to which questions we ask about our mission" is precisely the sort of idea that this book seeks to expand on (Gardner and Ramsey 2005, 33).

THEORETICAL FRAMES

Throughout this book are repeated references to particular theorists who have been instrumental in my critique of the writing center grand narrative; their ideas have given me language to articulate my argument. For the study of narratives, I'm influenced by the approach articulated by psychologist and cognitive learning theorist Jerome Bruner, who takes a constructivist view of narrative: "a view that takes as its central premise that 'world-making' is the principal function of the mind" (Bruner 2004, 28). Constructivists believe when we confront new information, in order to make sense of it we map it onto existing knowledge we have. This is how we make sense of the world, by linking new experiences to something else we already "know." So, for example, when I use a technology like a new computer, I use my past experiences with computers to negotiate the new one. Sometimes this existing knowledge aids us in figuring out the new information, sometimes it does not. For example, when a graduate student moves from being an Assistant Director of a writing center to a job as a tenure-track Writing Center Director, some of what she or he knows will map easily onto the new job. However, some things in the new context may be radically different; so, although the student-cum-director "knows" writing center work, she or he might feel a bit unfettered.

For Jerome Bruner, we make sense of the world through stories we internalize and externalize. Humans, he believes, have a strong impulse toward narrative, which is evident in how people form their life stories.

He believes that for humans, prior knowledge is often storied for our own comprehension and others', and as a constructivist, he thinks that when new events happen or new information comes to us, we try to fit it into our existing stories. Since my concern in this book is with how writing centers are storied, I am interested in how individual stories match (or do not match) the collective or community narrative. Bruner's work is helpful in looking at those intersections.

Three components of Bruner's ideas about narrative are particularly helpful for my undertaking, and I'll draw upon them throughout this book to talk in terms of community narratives, specifically writing center narratives. The first of these is Bruner's idea that an individual's narrative, or autobiography as he sometimes calls it, conforms to cultural expectations. He describes how telling our own story "is an act of 'entrenchment' to use Nelson Goodman's term. That is to say, we wish to present ourselves to others (and to ourselves) as typical or characteristic or 'culture confirming' in some way" (Bruner 1991a, 29).[1] In other words, narratives reveal how tellers are trying to belong. To suggest in writing scholarship writers aim to show their belonging to a discipline is not a radical notion. But to suggest that a longing to belong might affect how we describe our centers or our work is more radical and is precisely what I suggest might be happening. Some of us, at least, often describe or narrate our centers and our work in ways that comply with the discipline's narrative over the material realities we confront daily.

The second idea of Bruner's that I will draw on is his contention that past, internalized narratives direct future actions. He explains that "the ways of telling and the ways of reconceptualizing that go with them become so habitual that they finally become recipes for structuring experience itself, for laying down routes into memory, for not only guiding the life narrative up to the present, but for directing it into the future" (Bruner 1991a, 36). As we plot new events onto our existing maps, our mind works to see how this new event is part of "our" story. Many involved in writing center work have internalized what I have called the writing center grand narrative and when confronted by new ideas, our instinct is to see how the new idea fits into our existing internalized, collective narrative. Failing this, we might reject ideas that we cannot place within our existing story of our work. For many, the move to online tutoring in the 1990s was a new idea that was hard to place. The writing center story told of students and tutors meeting

1.   This idea strikes me as similar to how Richard Rorty, as discussed in Bruffee (1984), describes how a discipline uses normal discourse.

together, face-to-face in cozy spaces over physical texts. The loss of the physical place, human bodies and voices, and physical texts have made some question how well online tutoring even fits with the writing center model (e.g., see Carpenter 2008). Some writing center practitioners were able to resolve themselves to online tutoring only when it looked more familiar—when it was able to capture human bodies and voices through audio-textual-visual tutoring (see Yergeau et al. 2008). In constructivist terms, they could map audio-textual-visual tutoring more easily onto traditional face-to-face tutoring and thereby audio-textual-visual tutoring began to make sense as part of the already established narrative.

The third idea of Bruner's that grounds this book is the idea that narratives are interpretations of reality. There is no objective reality that is revealed in a narrative. He writes: "There is no innocent eye, nor is there one that penetrates aboriginal reality. There are instead hypotheses, versions, expected scenarios. Our precommitment about the nature of life is that it is a story, some narrative however put together. Perhaps we can say one other thing: any story one may tell about anything is better understood by considering other possible ways in which it can be told" (Bruner 1991a, 36). In other words, something called "reality" is not simply and unproblematically retold in a story. A story can have many versions, all of which, in some way or another, reflect "reality." Moreover, Bruner writes, "I have argued that a life as led is inseparable from a life as told—or more bluntly, a life is not 'how it was' but how it is interpreted and reinterpreted, told and retold" (36). In this vein, I think Bruner can show how there is not a singular way to talk about writing center work; instead, we can and should consider how writing centers are storied, what versions abound and what versions are suppressed, acknowledging that no story is innocent.

These three ideas—that narratives are culturally conforming, that past narratives shape future narratives, and that narratives are interpretations—undergird my readings of narrative in this book. In particular, my contention is that the writing center grand narrative is a collective story that individuals have in mind as they craft their own writing center stories. The writing center grand narrative sets the cultural standard to which individuals try to conform. Moreover, the writing center grand narrative as a collective narrative is internalized and shapes future narratives. Individuals try to make new events and experiences cohere with the past—the established story of writing center work—in order to make the narrative legible as a writing center story. Finally, reading the writing center grand narrative with the perception that it is a version—one of infinite possible tellings—loosens the powerful grip of the writing center grand narrative. The main objective of this book, then, is to show how the writing center grand narrative as a collective, internalized story shapes writing center discourse and that seeing this story as dominant but not comprehensive allows us to change writing center work and discourse. To this end, I look for narratives that correspond with the writing center grand narrative, that reify it, and that diverge from it.

Along with Bruner, another theorist who plays predominantly into my thinking is Kris Fleckenstein. As I attempt to show how stories shape how we look at the world, I draw on Fleckenstein's ideas in *Vision, Rhetoric, and Social Action in the Composition Classroom,* where she shows the interconnectedness of rhetorical habits and visual habits, of what we say and what we perceive. While rhetorical habits "provide protocols for engagement with and performance of certain social actions" (Fleckenstein 2010, 8), visual habits are "systems of perception that, through an array of habitualized conventions, organize reality in particular ways, leading us to discern some images and not others, to relate those images in characteristic ways to each other and ourselves, and to link those images to language in a uniform dynamic" (10). Fleckenstein further explains "a visual habit works as a reality sieve or a set of blinders, directing our attention to some facets of reality while rendering others invisible" (10). In short, rhetorical habits are patterns of language use and visual habits are ways of seeing. These are interdependent: the ways we use language condition the ways we see and vice versa.

For Fleckenstein, we belong to communities in proportion to the degree in which we can participate in specific visual and rhetorical modes valued by that community: "Membership in a culture is predicated on one's ability to see and speak in the privileged mode. To be a member of a particular culture demands that one develop and deploy that culture's dominant way of seeing and speaking. Acquired through participation in cultural activities with cultural artifacts, ways of seeing feed back into what images can be perceived and, thus, what god images can develop" (Fleckenstein 2010, 10–11). What I'm arguing here is that the ways we talk about writing centers affect what we see and don't see in writing centers, what work we value and don't value. Second, as connected to Fleckenstein's ideas about community, writing center professionals coalesce to very specific rhetorical and visual habits, and participating in the community of writing center professionals consequently means participating in the shared rhetorical and visual habits.

Finally, though Nancy Grimm would probably not characterize her approach to writing center scholarship as strictly narrative critique, her influence on this book is obvious. In all that Grimm writes, she pushes writing center professionals to closely examine our practices and most cherished, entrenched beliefs. In "The Regulatory Role of Writing Centers," for instance, she uses the analogy of stripping wood to describe her goal of stripping away rhetoric "we have developed to explain what happens in writing centers" (Grimm 1996b, 5). She explains how this is painful yet productive when she writes, "My goal is to fully position writing centers in the painful paradoxes of literacy work, to strip away the belief in innocence in order to make us more fully aware of the ways that literacy practices reproduce the social order and regulate access and subjectivity" (5). Grimm's work again and again asks me to scrutinize what I think I know about writing center work and the representation of it.

Grimm confirms for me that one can be—and perhaps ought to be— an ardent believer in writing centers and also a tireless critic. She interrogates sacred practices and ideas—even in writing center scholarship, the place where the writing center grand narrative is often invoked. She writes that "research in the writing center can examine those struggles and emerge with a more critical sense of the effect of our curriculum and teaching practices, but often it doesn't. If we think of the nature of our work as neutral, value-free and institutionally sanctioned, we are more likely to focus our research on how we can help students write better assignments, how we can train tutors to be more effective at helping students write better assignments, how we can improve our image and promote our services" (Grimm 1992, 5). In other words, our perceptions and representations of writing centers predispose us to think about research problems and research agendas in certain ways. So if the writing center grand narrative tells a story of pluck and love, then it may lead us to more research on how we can be more ingenious or more loving in our work. This conception—or any conception—will direct how we enter into scholarly conversations, will direct the rhetorical and visual habits of the scholarly community. Grimm gives permission and instruction to turn a critical eye to the storying of writing center work.

In the next three chapters, I use the lenses provided by narrative theory to interrogate stories about writing center work. I look at pieces of the writing center grand narrative, isolating the iterations of the story, thinking through the consequences of the telling of the story, and considering alternative peripheral stories and visions.

3

WRITING CENTERS ARE COZY HOMES

To the extent that writing centers believe not only in the neutrality of their work, but also take comfort in the worn couches and homelike ambiance of their work sites, to the extent that they theorize themselves as institutionalized sites of service and individualized instruction, they are participating in the regulatory uses of literacy.
—Nancy Grimm (1996), "The Regulatory Role of
the Writing Center"

Every story needs a setting, a place for the action to happen. Part of what distinguishes writing center work from composition more generally is the site; writing can happen anywhere, but writing center work implies a set location—a writing center. This chapter is about the setting for the writing center grand narrative: the physical centers we inhabit and the ways in which we discourse or narrate them. Of all the pieces of the writing center grand narrative, I think the idea that a writing center is—and should be—a cozy, homey, comfortable, family-like place is perhaps most firmly entrenched. As I wrote in the introduction, the argument in this book is that writing center work is complex, although the storying of it often is not. The same issue holds true for writing center spaces: many stories could be told of our spaces, yet predominately, one story is told.

In this chapter then, I discuss how the storying of writing centers as cozy places came to be. Using Bruner's ideas of constructivist narrative, I show how past stories direct more recent ones and how composing the "writing center space as cozy home" narrative is a culturally conforming act even as it defies local, material conditions. In the last part of this chapter, I discuss how the lenses of critical geography and cultural materialism help produce stories with more dissonance, which is another way for us to move away from our conditioned patterns of seeing and not seeing.

To begin, consider this thread on the WCENTER listserv. A new director described her somewhat fortunate problem of having to design a writing center from scratch. She ended her post with these questions:

"If you could have anything you wanted in a Writing Center facility, what would it be? And what could you not live without?" (England 2005). She received several similar replies, such as this one:

Indispensable things in my humble opinion are

- Round tables
- Art
- Plants
- A window to stare out
- Bookshelves
- Coffee pot
- Decent chairs
- Couches (Gardner 2005)

Other replies listed some of the same "indispensable things." Reading this discussion, I was reminded how many of these objects are familiar to writing center professionals as "must haves." Specifically, descriptions of writing center spaces often mention round tables, art, plants, couches, and coffee pots with such frequency that these objects almost become iconic. In fact, in Joyce Kinkead and Jeanette Harris's collection of twelve writing center "case studies," the closest thing to a common denominator connecting the diverse centers is the coffee pot—not philosophies of writing, not methods for tutor training, but the presence of a coffee pot. They note: "As we read these descriptions, every once in a while we think we come across a characteristic that crosses the board. Coffee—instant, brewed, or café latte—seems almost universal" (Kinkead and Harris 1993, 236). What is it about coffee pots and these other objects? How have they become so intertwined with writing center identity?

To be legible, indeed, to be read as a writing center, a space needs to have a particular array of objects. Most spaces are like this. Users have expectations about what a space will have in it and what it won't have. For instance, we expect a waiting room at the doctor's office or at the auto shop will have uncomfortable chairs very close together and pushed against the walls, magazines, a few toys, and perhaps a TV on a news channel with the volume low. When we see a space like this, its arrangement tells us we can wait there. Through their arrangements and objects, spaces communicate to us; we could even say that spaces tell us a story about what they are and how we may use them. Or as Harry Denny puts it, spaces perform (Denny 2010, 153). Having couches or photos or coffee pots reveals an effort to construct a space different from classrooms and other impersonal, institutional spaces.[1]

Writing center practitioners and scholars, in fact, contend with ideas of space and design frequently since writing centers typically have been space-bound. Unlike some composition teachers who may teach in different sites each hour, day, and semester, writing center professionals return to the same space each day. Perhaps this is why many of the metaphors for writing center work are place-related such as Andrea Lunsford's (2001) garret, storehouse, Burkean parlor; Elizabeth Boquet's (1999) laundry or safe house; Stephen North's skills center, fix-it shop, or "cross between Lourdes and a hospice" (North 1984, 65); or Denny's (2010) clubhouse.

Though it is certainly desirable for writing centers to be legible to users, it is curious of all the possible stories how the idea of a writing center as cozy home became dominant. It is fairly common to find in descriptions of writing centers the objects and arrangements that writers believe communicate a metaphor of home: this writing center is comfortable, inviting, and just like home. Take, for instance, these descriptions of centers:

> JOHNSON COMMUNITY COUNTY COLLEGE: "Although somewhat crowded with numerous bookcases, filing cabinets, and vertical files, the room's most noticeable features are the friendly faces seated at round tables throughout the room.
> "The furniture was selected to create a comfortable learning environment, and colorful posters and plants help to put the visiting student at ease." (Mohr 1993, 148)

> PURDUE: "All of [what we've put in our center] signal (we hope) that this mess is also a friendly, nonthreatening, nonclassroom environment where conversation and questions can fly from one table to another." (Harris 1993, 5–6)

> HARVARD: "Our furniture is comfortable and inviting, with two couches and several chairs in the reception area, rugs in all offices, and attractive posters on the wall." (Simon 1993, 118)

> AN "IDEAL" CENTER: "The room is comfortable, with familiar eight-foot ceilings; light, calming colors; soft carpet; plants, and soft lighting—provided by cove lighting and a skylight." (Hadfield et al. 2003, 171)

> LEHIGH UNIVERSITY: "The plants, as well as the high ceiling and comfortable furniture, help create a welcoming atmosphere." (Lotto 1993, 85)

---

1. Inman argues, "Many centers appear to have been designed around furnishings and technologies rather than what clients will actually be doing" (Inman 2010, 20). Instead, he proposes a concept of zoning for space design.

In each of these, the writers make a direct connection between objects or arrangement and meaning that is shown in the adjectives: soft, calming, welcoming, comfortable, attractive, familiar, non-threatening, and friendly. Describing a writing center space in this way is not unique; it happens so often it has probably become transparent, something we no longer pay much attention to. Jerome Bruner calls this sort of thing narrative accrual—stories pile up, so to speak—and when they do "the accruals eventually create something variously called a 'culture' or a 'history' or, more loosely, a 'tradition'" (Bruner 1991b, 18). Each time another writing center practitioner describes his or her writing center in line with the writing center grand narrative, that story bolsters the tradition.

The dominance of the narrative of the cozy home can be traced back to conscious decisions made by writing center directors to bring objects and arrangement to centers to make the space look like home. They wanted to create a physical identity for the center that welcomed students and comforted them. Boquet notes the move toward the homey decor was a conscious move away from the early auto-tutorial writing labs. The desire not to be the skill-and-drill lab led directors to "characterize the lab spaces as non-threatening (however specious) and to fill them with creature comforts—couches, plants, coffee pots, posters" (Boquet 1999, 51). For instance, included in the IWCA's online toolkit for those interested in starting a new writing center is Muriel Harris's "SLATE Statement: The Concept of a Writing Center." In this statement Harris recommends accounting for the following in a budget: "To ensure that the writing center is an informal, friendly place, the room benefits from plants, a coffee pot, tables where students can sit side-by-side, and dictionaries and other reference books to use while writing" (Harris 1988, par. 33). Here we see unequivocal advice on how to set the mood (buy plants and a coffee pot) and why (to ensure an informal and friendly place).

Besides just a decision to be "friendly," another reason writing centers try to compose themselves as cozy homes is, as Peter Carino supposes, that a writing center envisions itself as family: "Writing centers are fond of seeing themselves in metaphors of family—cozy homes with soft couches where when students go they must be taken in" (Carino 1995a, 20). Furthermore, as Boquet observes, tutors came and made themselves at home: "Students ceased to simply visit the writing center; they began, with the advent of peer tutoring, to inhabit it, to hang hand-lettered renditions of their favorite quotations on the wall, to jot down jokes on the board, to leave their own work on the tables while answering a question" (Boquet 1999, 53). It is evident in writing center research and lore that having a "homey" writing center is not unique, nor is it accidental. Professionals in the field created friendly centers, or what they imagined were friendly centers, for conscious reasons; they did not want to be that other, scary institutional lab for remedial students; they wanted students to feel welcome and like one big family. Writing centers wanted to assure students that nothing would be done to them upon entering—the centers were less doctor's office or science lab and more like any old living room. The way to send this message to students was to add and arrange objects in ways that evoke home.

Interestingly, as writing centers move increasingly to virtual spaces for online consulting, there is a stated desire for the online tutoring setting to be homey—to mimic the narrative of the physical writing center setting. For example in "Consultations without Bodies: Technology, Virtual Space, and the Writing Center," Rusty Carpenter asks if our virtual tutoring is comparable to our physical writing centers, which he sees as an example of Ray Oldenburg's "great good place": "The writing center, in many ways, tries to replicate these cozy spaces, providing a place for students to feel a sense of community with other interested writers. Some writing centers provide coffee or snacks, while others simply provide a relaxing and supportive atmosphere that promotes conversation. In large part, writing centers have embraced the role of the 'great good place,' although the inviting ambiance and personality do not always come across in virtual spaces. With the growing number of Online Writing Labs (OWLs), how do we convey the inviting and supporting aura in our virtual spaces and consultations?" (Carpenter 2008). The question he isn't asking but that seems to be perplexing him is, how can we describe our centers without relying on the story we typically use?

I, for one, wonder about this recipe: (1) take a space; (2) add a coffee pot, posters, couch, and plants; (3) relish your friendly, non-threatening, comfortable center. Sure, I think having some of these items marks a space as a non-classroom space, but I've seen far too many uncomfortable people in writing centers to believe that this is all it takes to make a space "comfortable." I'm afraid writing center professionals use these descriptions to show themselves as insiders in the field of writing centers—to show that they know the writing center grand narrative— rather than to really describe the feel of a space. As Bruner reminds us, even if we don't intend to, we necessarily draw on the cultural norms when we try to make meaning. He writes that "the symbolic systems that individuals used in constructing meaning were systems that were already in place, already 'there,' deeply entrenched in culture and language" (Bruner 1990, 11). Doing so, using the symbolic systems of our culture, makes the users "a reflection of the community" (11).

DECONSTRUCTING THE HOME

Thinking of our writing centers as cozy homes, insisting on them as such in our discourse and scholarship, can certainly make us feel good. It can buttress our sense that writing centers are anti-academic, anti-establishment, caring, and iconoclastic. But, as Beth Daniell warns, we ought to "be careful of literacy narratives that make us feel good" (Daniell 1999, 401). In this next section, I want to turn toward the consequences of storying our centers as cozy homes.

To begin, one problem is the fact that homes are culturally marked. If a writing center is a home, whose home is it? Mine? Yours? For whom is it comfortable? Everyone, likely more than once, has entered another person's home and immediately felt uncomfortable, however welcoming the host or however strong our desire to be there. Growing up, this feeling was strongest for me when my family went to rural Nebraska to visit my grandparents. On the farm, typical rules were relaxed; my brothers and I could run off and return hours later, we didn't watch for traffic, we didn't have to stay clean. Yet as the city kids, we always felt a bit awkward. We were certainly more squeamish around farm life than my cousins who lived there—we were the target of laughter as we recoiled at the ever-present stench of manure, gathered eggs from underneath attacking hens, and watched Grandpa slaughter a hog.

Like it or not, when we fill our writing centers with touches of home, we may be marking it as familiar and comfortable for directors and tutors, who are often, as Nancy Grimm (1999) points out, of a certain class (upper or middle class) and cultural background (white American). Abstract art on the walls might seem pretentious to those who grew up in homes with family photos and pre-framed nature or religious prints from discount stores. We might recreate the familiar patterns of our class or culture's idea of home: guests are greeted at the front door, led to a sitting room or table for dining, escorted back to the front door after the visit, and asked to return. These patterns might not be shared by all students particularly in writing centers when our clientele might include a greater proportion of students who are not white or privileged or American than the general university population. Grimm notes that the very adjective "*comfortable* is frequently associated with America's vast middle class" (Grimm 1999, 115, italics in original).

Calling oneself "comfortable" is a way of aligning with mainstream values. Once aligned as such, the middle class protects that comfort by "avoiding situations that produce discomfort, turning to indirect communication when situations make us uncomfortable, and inadvertently sidelining the people who make us uncomfortable" (115).

Another issue we ought to be mindful of is that for some students (and perhaps some directors and tutors as well), school is an escape from home. Home life may be abusive or dangerous. Intellectual pursuits may be misunderstood or discouraged, and basic needs might not be met. Or, in less extreme situations, home just might not be a good place to get work done. The TV is too loud or too enticing, the puppy or kids too needy, or the apartment too small or too messy to think. We imagine that students use the writing center as an alternative to the institution, but I wonder how many also use the writing center as an alternative to the home.

Furthermore, one cannot ignore the gender implications in making a writing center feel like home. Historically in Western culture the home was the sphere of the female, the wife. Likewise, both composition studies at large and writing center work in particular have been the realm of women (see Nicolas 2004, 2007; Holbrook 1991; Miller 2003). Women disproportionately hold positions as composition teachers, writing program administrators, and writing center directors. It could be argued that writing centers, often started by women, were designed as a female space in opposition to the institution at large, which was male, uncomfortable, foreign. This would constitute an internal assertion of identity. Or, alternatively, writing center spaces could be gendered female by outsiders based on the gender of the director or the feminization of the field at large. Melissa Nicolas thinks writing centers are feminized because "we are seen as nurturing, service-oriented places" (Nicolas 2004, 12). For Nicolas, this is problematic since this "feminization of the writing center narrative" functions to "code the position of the writing center director as 'inferior,' regardless of rank" (12). Whether female directors have tried to carve a safe haven in a male institution by making themselves homes in the writing center (an argument I'm not prepared to make) or centers have been labeled "feminine" and thus seen as inferior by others, clinging to the identity of a writing center as cozy home may be problematic in terms of gender. Female directors who insist on cozy, inviting spaces may be unwittingly narrating their work as nonintellectual in the eyes of some. Fact is, if the writing center is home and staff is family, that makes the director the mother.

This is not to say that writing centers should not be spaces to carry out the work of feminism; they can be. Such work does not have to be "comfortable" though and, in fact, might work better if it is confrontational and unsettling. Susan Jarratt tells us writing classrooms do not have to be nurturing: "For some composition teachers, creating a supportive climate in the classroom and validating student experience leads them to avoid conflict" (Jarratt 2003, 263–64). Conflict is not to be avoided but engaged to prepare students for lives outside of their classrooms. Working through conflict can teach students how to use a public voice (277). If writing centers are imagined as homes, they are consciously constructed as private spaces where writers can retreat. Students will not get practice using a public voice or engaging in public discourse if the tutoring is carefully crafted to nurture. Furthermore, Jarratt states, "differences of gender, race, and class among students and teachers provide situations in which conflict does arise, and we need more than the ideal of the harmonious, nurturing composition class in our repertory of teaching practices to deal with these problems" (271). Perhaps writing centers need other ideals as well.

Likewise, bell hooks describes a different kind of feminist space— one that does not nurture but works because of the confrontations and exchange of ideas. Of this, she writes: "Suddenly, the feminist classroom is no longer a safe haven, the way many women's studies students imagine it will be, but instead is a site of conflict, tensions, and sometimes ongoing hostility. Confronting one another across differences means that we must change ideas about how we learn; rather than fearing conflict, we have to find ways to use it as a catalyst for new thinking, for growth" (hooks 1994, 113). These ideas about feminist classrooms that are not homes or safe havens, yet nonetheless effective, could translate to writing centers. Writing centers already make students uncomfortable—they make students revise, confront their shortcomings, formulate questions, engage us in their work, be active, and think. A homey center may work against the job writing centers want to do. Couches, beanbag chairs, pillows, low lights, and lava lamps may put students in the mood to lounge, sit back, relax. It may not communicate to students that they will need to be active agents in the tutoring session if it's going to work. Writing centers may unwittingly be putting too much emphasis on the affective dimension of tutoring, in an effort to get more students to use their centers, instead of the intellectual. We shortchange our students if we doubt that they are interested in serious intellectual conversations.

TOWARD PERIPHERAL VISIONS OF WRITING CENTER SPACES

Thus far, I've argued that the idea of a writing center as a cozy place is a key part of the grand narrative of writing centers. It is often repeated and thus reinforced by writing center scholars and practitioners. The repeated tellings of the writing center as home has the potential consequence of obscuring complicated practices of culture, class, and gender written on notions of "home" and "comfortable." However, up to this point, I've more or less believed the narrative to be true: that writing centers are or intend to be cozy. Writing center scholars and practitioners consciously design their spaces to be homey and report on how they've done this in writing center scholarship.

In this final section, though, I put on my doubting hat. I suggest that the need to tell a story compatible with the writing center grand narrative leads writing center scholars to talk about their centers in terms of home rather than in some other way. Bruner says that "narratives are a version of reality whose acceptability is governed by convention and 'narrative necessity' rather than by empirical verification and logical requiredness" (Bruner 1991b, 4). Therefore, we don't hold stories to the same burden of truth; they don't have to correspond with reality. "Narrative 'truth,'" Bruner suggests, "is judged by its verisimilitude rather than its verifiability. There seems indeed to be some sense in which narrative, rather than referring to 'reality,' may in fact create or constitute it" (13). Though I do not want to suggest that a story could or ought to report just the facts of a reality out there (that sort of thing just isn't possible), I do want to spend some time in this last part of the chapter looking at how critical geography and cultural materialism might expand our field of vision beyond the tunnel vision (or blindness) created by unthoughtful adherence to the writing center grand narrative.

In her article "Composition's Imagined Geographies," Nedra Reynolds asks compositionists to look at the material realities of where writing happens instead of looking through it. She employs postmodern geography "to explore how spaces and places are socially produced through discourse, and how these constructed places can deny their connections to material reality or mask material conditions" (Reynolds 1998, 13). Reynolds asserts that the field depends more on spatial metaphors (specifically composition as frontier, city, or cyberspace) to describe where writing happens rather than qualitative descriptions of actual writing spaces. This work is of obvious significance to writing center professionals. If the writing center as home is part of the grand narrative for writing centers, then it is easy to see how this spatial meta-phor may distract us from the material realities of actual writing cen-ters. For example, while describing a center as having a couch and softly painted walls may invoke the metaphor of home for some readers of that description, a wider, more critical reading of a space may reveal a much different mood—what if the couch is terribly stiff, the walls a dirty beige, and the center itself full of self-righteous tutors?

Reynolds believes "a geographic emphasis would insist on more atten-tion to the connections between spaces and practices, more effort to link the material conditions to the activities of particular spaces" (Reynolds 1998, 30). This is not likely the same type of geographic study that we may have learned in high school. According to critical geographer Tim Cresswell, the study of geography has changed dramatically in recent decades: "The direction of recent critical geography has been away from seeing its object as the description of regions and toward the analysis of the role of geographic forces in the explanation of other things" (Cresswell 1996, 12). In other words, the work is no longer just stat-ing this place has *x*; it is about explaining human patterns of behavior, for one, based on a place having *x*. In terms of the writing center, criti-cal geographies would not merely state what objects occupy the space. In addition, the focus would include the human experience in use of space and objects. For example, it is one thing to have a coffee pot, it is another thing to have a coffee pot that is so grimy that no one uses it and cleaning it becomes a source of tension among tutors. Furthermore, critical geographers see the landscape as a text that "is subject to mul-tiple readings despite the fact that some readings are encouraged more than others" (Cresswell 1996, 13). If the favorable reading of writing centers is writing center as home, it is crucial to know what readings are not encouraged or suppressed in our literature.

Reading a writing center also means reading the objects within those spaces; the work of cultural materialists show us how this is possible and what can result. For W. David Kingery, cultural materialism is the focus on objects "as evidence to be interpreted" (Kingery 1996, 2). He believes that reading objects is even more difficult than reading texts: "No one denies the importance of things, but learning from them requires rather more attention than reading texts. The grammar of things is related to, but more complex and difficult to decipher than, the grammar of words. Artifacts are tools as well as signals, signs, and symbols" (1). Whether truly more difficult or not—he surely would meet with contestation uttering this at MLA—thinking of objects as open to interpretation with many possible meanings interrupts our steady narratives of, say, the coffee pot as necessarily a symbol of friendliness or comfort. Interestingly enough, both approaches are asking for a sort of textual analysis—something most writing center professionals are pretty familiar with. A critical geographer's eye or cultural materialist's lens won't help us see conclusively what our centers say or what they mean. Instead, these approaches ask us to be open to the surplus of meanings that are contained in any space or with any object, and they ask us to question what readings may be privileged.

An example of how writing center spaces can be read differently by different people can be found in Colleen Connolly, Amy DeJarlais, Alice Gillam, and Laura Micciche's article "Erika and the Fish Lamps: Writing and Reading the Local Scene." In this piece, the authors describe the writing center scene at the University of Wisconsin, Milwaukee. They trace (actually, mourn) the change in décor when a new administrator comes to office. Initially, the center is painted a pale rose and houses battered easy chairs, fish lamps, a punk mannequin head (named Erika), artwork, signs, knickknacks, a clock, and a stereo that plays cool jazz. Of this décor, the authors note, "Consciously or unconsciously, we were marking the standard institutional space we were issued as different from other institutional spaces, as nongeneric, unconventional, eclectic, in, but not altogether of, the larger academy" (Connolly et al. 1998, 18). In addition, as they describe specific elements of their center, more of their "marking" appears. For one, they describe the lamps as "a welcoming relief from the harsh fluorescent lights in most classrooms" (19). And overall, they see, "the decorations and easygoing atmosphere announced the center's alternative identity and student-centered approach to writing conferences" (19). These descriptions are infused with the authors' reading of these spaces. The lamps are good—"welcoming"; the fluorescents are bad—"harsh." To the authors, the tutor-created décor communicated an identity—"easy going . . . student-centered."

Conflict brews when the new administrator does not share this reading of the space. She turns the fluorescent lights on, throws out Erika and the easy chairs, and turns off the jazz. After these changes the veteran tutors are disheartened, yet the students who use the center "appear generally unaffected" (20). In the end, the authors are forced to question their reading of the space. While they read their original arrangement and decoration of space as "student-centered," students themselves still saw the center as comfortable and friendly after the new director changed it. In reflection, the authors ask, "Did tutor culture sometimes take precedence over service to students? Was our funky style an end in itself rather than a means to a larger pedagogical purpose?" (25). This sort of questioning is important because it is the start of a more critical reading of writing center spaces; the authors see how the contested interpretation of the space and artifacts changed the working conditions for the tutors and thus changed how writing instruction took place. Their focus was not a list of the objects in the center but readings of how students and tutors used the space both before and after the changes to décor.

Contrast this with "An Ideal Writing Center" by Leslie Hadfield, Joyce Kinkead, Tom Peterson, Stephanie Ray, and Sarah Preston, which puts forward an uncritical reading of a writing center space. In this article, the authors set forth on a project to imagine an ideal center for an imaginary university, Alchemy U. Although the undertaking of this project seems odd given that it is widely agreed that context is of paramount importance in guiding writing center practice, their plan is nonetheless interesting. The interdisciplinary team wisely used design theory to create a space that would meet the needs of the imagined institution. The center would be 4,813 total square feet, split nearly evenly between a "main area" and computer lab. The main area would have many of the same objects noted in other writing centers: carpet, soft lighting, plants, comfortable sofa, and round tables.

This article's review of types of classroom design and architecture is useful; however, the authors fall into the same trap as many other writing center designers—they force a particular reading on their plan as if it is the only possible reading. According to the authors, "the environment that we developed for an ideal writing center is calm, non-threatening, and easily understood" (Hadfield et al. 2003, 171), and "the design conveys to students that the writing center is a place where they can receive help without the pressure that comes with a classroom environment" (175). While this is an imaginary plan and the authors cannot see how users actually interact with the space and report on the use of the space, the authors could still give a more critical reading by acknowledging the possibility of other readings of the plan. Instead, the authors come to a rather absurd claim after interviewing those who work in and use an existing writing center: "All three groups—tutors, students, and staff—share common ideas about what makes an ideal writing center" (171). This makes me wonder how much the privileged narrative of writing centers, of writing centers as homes, influenced the authors' plan and interviewing of users. I can believe that many users may have similar ideas about what would make a good writing center, especially users privy to writing center literature that more or less prescribes a certain type of center; however, I also believe that many ideas that came forth in the interviews of tutors, students, and staff must have been glossed over or simply ignored.

I come to this conclusion after hearing my graduate students quite passionately discuss this piece in a seminar titled "Comp without Classrooms." In that class, we discussed some of composition's alternative sites: writing centers, service learning sites, and online learning. Prior to the class, only one student had experience tutoring in a writing center. One or two had sent students to the writing center, but otherwise all others were reading about and engaging writing center issues for the first time. In fact, for several students, this was the first graduate course in composition they had ever taken, so they were coming to the conversation as beginners. One Friday, we spent the better part of an hour discussing the layout of Hadfield et al.'s imaginary space; our interpretations of the authors' plan for an ideal center widely varied. One student, Clyde, liked that there was a room for everything, everything had a place. He explained that his family had outgrown their house, and with his wife having a business based at home and he and his children trying to study, all the clutter at home drove him crazy. Others felt it was not the sort of place that would inspire writing. Annie, a high school English teacher and poet, was appalled by the straight lines and in-the-box thinking of the plan. If it is an ideal center, why not create a space where writers would gravitate, she wondered. She desired curved walls, a set of French doors that opened onto a patio complete with fountain, of course. After all, she reminded us, the authors did claim their design to be an ideal center.

Of particular debate were the tutoring rooms. In the plan, there are four small rooms set aside for one-to-one tutoring across from the director's office. Some of my students liked the professional ethos it lends to tutoring—it seems important and valued if it gets its own office. Yet others, including me, were weary of the small rooms. From my work with sexual assault victims, I'm sensitive to the fact that sitting in a closed-door, small office with a stranger is not comfortable for some people. Jessica, the former tutor, added that she preferred an open room for tutoring.

The other hot topic was the location of the director's office directly across from the tutoring rooms. The authors of the article note that "the director requested an office that is central" (Hadfield et al. 2003, 173). Since this person must "be all, see all, and hear all," they gave the director an office with windows to the outside and windows that give a view of most of the main room (173). Many of my students wondered how this might jeopardize the important peer-to-peer relationship in tutoring they had been reading about. I immediately thought of the first writing center that I worked at, which had an office for the director right in the center. The new faculty director (wisely, I think) asked for an office outside of the center. She did not want to see all or hear all, nor be always readily available. I wondered how I would ever get any writing done or how I would deal with the lack of privacy that having a glass office would offer. Clearly, my concerns were different than those of the director interviewed for the project, illustrating again that spaces can be read differently.

The "ideal center" is a paper plan, quite literally a text, which perhaps invited critique by asserting itself as "ideal" in the first place. In our field, we may be less likely to question a reading/writing of space or object when the author has firsthand experience with it, but we should question it when the reading seems to leave something out. Researchers should aim to write about spaces in a way that showcases spaces in all of their complexity by not allowing their own interpretation of the space to be the only reading. According to Gesa Kirsch and Joy Ritchie, dissonances in our research should not be frightening: "Researchers cannot escape a position of power and the potential for appropriating or manipulating information. The point here, however, is not to suggest that scholars ignore or omit data that seem to contradict their views. Rather, the point is to encourage researchers to view dissonances as opportunities to examine deeply held assumptions and to allow multiple voices to emerge in their research studies, an act that will require innovation in writing research reports" (Kirsch and Ritchie 1995, 19). Critical readings reveal what shorthand descriptions don't. Connolly et al. provide a critical reading of their center despite the messiness of it. It would have been a neater narrative—and probably more personally satisfying—for the authors to trace their deep satisfaction with the space before the new director and their feelings of loss of community and identity when the space changed. But instead of relying on the easy narrative, the authors complicate this with the readings from the student perspective, a peripheral vision. They show that the students kept coming to the center even after the space had changed. Their article highlights the dissonances that the ideal writing center article masks.

Throughout this chapter, I have tried to establish that many writing center scholars and practitioners are working under the same assumption about their writing centers that may be put into question by others' interpretations and by deconstructing their ideals. The writing center grand narrative that writes writing centers as homes has taught us to narrow our gaze, to see particular items and to ignore others. Peripheral vision asks us to widen our view. Doing so, I might notice, for example, that what gets used most in my writing center, what is indeed indispensable for us, include computers, Kleenex, a stapler, cleaning spray, pencils, trash cans, breath mints, bulletin boards, our telephone, forms, the front desk, a coat rack, and our worn copies of the *Everyday Writer* handbook. These items don't tell a coherent story of another place; they certainly don't remind me of home. Yet, these items do tell the story of our particular writing center if we're interested in listening.

We can begin to re-see our centers if we look *at* our spaces as opposed to *through* them. Although all descriptions are shorthand, are in flux, are undetermined and overdetermined, just as all writing centers are, we can work toward a narrative that allows for multiple interpretations, thick descriptions, and even dissonance. What we ought to stop doing is using descriptions to fortify a narrative of cozy homes simply because it allows us to imagine that our spaces are (or should be) friendly or that writing about our centers in particular ways marks us as belonging to the writing center culture.

4

WRITING CENTERS ARE ICONOCLASTIC

Sometimes we just fall in love with lies.
—Cornel West, Twitter post, 29 November 2010

I don't think it is outside the realm of possibility that someone will eventually set a TV series or movie on a college campus with a character who works at a writing center. For years, characters have worked for the school newspaper, which revealed to the audience their earnest nerdiness. And now that writing centers have become fixtures at colleges, it seems inevitable that a writing center tutor could be next. Characters who are written as cheerleaders or jocks are typically shallow, mean, wealthy, and/or dull. But what would the qualities of the writing center tutor stock character be? What would working in the writing center reveal about a character?

If a scriptwriter went to a writing center conference or read much writing center scholarship, he or she might well come up with a character who was smart yet insolent. Someone who went to a college but was not part of the college—someone who doesn't know the name of the football team's quarterback, doesn't own a hoodie or bumper sticker with the school logo, but one who is on a first-name basis with the reference librarian, runs the student Greenpeace chapter, and whose best friend is the town's record-shop owner. There is a type of student who seems to find his or her way into writing centers as a tutor and a type of professional who is drawn to writing center administration, and I don't think this is accidental. Throughout writing center scholarship is an ongoing notion that writing center work is different, non-traditional— iconoclastic—and thus those who work there are, too. Thus, the image of a "typical" writing center tutor or administrator can become a visual habit, something we are accustomed to seeing and looking for and can lock us in a pattern of expectation and fulfillment. We might, for instance, (un)consciously hire or recruit tutors or administrators who seem a "good fit."

For instance, Andrew Rihn describes what drew him to writing center work in "Resistance One-on-One." He writes:

> I am a conflicted person by nature. I don't often feel like I fit in, even in places where I really want to. I feel like a charlatan, an impostor, because I am always critiquing the very institutions I become a part of. This facet of my personality leads me to seek out other people and places that don't quite belong, spaces that represent the "borderland," people with whom I can share my sense of "in-betweeness." Maybe these impulses were what first led me to my campus Writing Center, where I have worked as a peer tutor for three years. (Rihn 2010, 20)

His story, I think, is *the* story.

The piece of the writing center grand narrative that I explore in this chapter is the idea of the writing center as iconoclastic. An iconoclast is someone who assails venerated institutions, historically churches. The writing center, instead, resists the university system as an institution. "Iconoclastic," though not used as frequently in the scholarship as "cozy," "friendly," or "homey," seems to me the best word to invoke the various descriptors of writing centers, writing center scholarship, and consequently writing center professionals that are used: alternative, insolent, rebellious, different, non-traditional, (not) marginal. The sense of the writing center, the scholarship, and the people who work there as non-traditional or anti-institutional certainly pervades other chapters of this book, particularly in the ideas that writing centers reject the dominant pedagogies and relationships encouraged in the institution and that writing center people compose their spaces in particular ways to mark them as non-traditional classroom spaces. Here, though, I focus on the positionality or belongingness of writing centers within their institutions and the status of writing center scholarship and administrators; this chapter is about how we came to tell the story of ourselves as outsiders on the inside and how that story has and has not served us.

Without a doubt the two most-cited, most ardently iconoclastic anthems in writing center scholarship are Terrance Riley's "The Unpromising Future of Writing Centers" and Kevin Davis's "Life Outside the Boundary." These two articles articulate the rebellious, iconoclastic status of writing center, scholarship, and writing center professionals. In his article, originally published in the *Writing Center Journal*, Riley states that making writing center studies into a discipline with theories, scholars, journals, associations, publications, and such is the undoing of writing centers. Instead, he believes that writing centers ought to be counterhegemonic to remain true to their origins. If writing centers become institutionalized, Riley claims, they will follow other ill-fated areas of study (like, he claims, American literature, critical theory, and composition studies) that "demonstrated that what they were doing was not being done by any other department or discipline; evolved theories and discourses that highlighted their differences from other areas, and increasingly wrote only for members of their network; they amassed a body of scholarship that looked a good deal like what everyone else was producing; and on these bases they claimed a professional status often and loudly enough that they were listened to" (Riley 1994, 147). Riley argues, writing centers must find a "purity of purpose": "Professional success is proportional to the degree to which a discipline can overcome its mixed descent and claim a purity of purpose, creating an environment in which its members can measure themselves according to criteria internal to the discipline" (147). Riley foresees a future, an unpromising one as his title suggests, in which "the future of writing centers is exactly in the mainstream of the university" (150). Riley would rather see a future where folks in writing centers hold their outsider, iconoclastic status. Our energy, he writes, comes from our "happy amateurism" (151).

Similarly, one year later, Kevin Davis's article was printed in *The Writing Lab Newsletter*. In a rather personal essay, Davis discloses how as an "insolent academic" he has found a home in the writing center: "I lived a life on the boundary. I had two choices: accept the indoctrination I spent my life avoiding, or finding an academic role that nurtured my insolence, idealism, and creativity. I found that role in a writing center" (Davis 1995, 6). (Note how similar this reads to Rihn's story, quoted earlier.) Here he says he is "paid to subvert academic stuffiness" (6). Like Riley, he does not want the writing center to become mainstream, instead choosing "carefully, purposefully—to keep the center firmly on the outside" (6). Moreover, he says: "And to be faithful to our legacies, the center and I must maintain our personalities as renegades, outsiders, boundary dwellers, subversives. Maybe, it now occurs to me, 'writing center' is the ultimate misnomer; maybe we should be called the 'writing outland'" (7).

In his closing, he offers three maxims to encourage other writing center directors to follow his lead. First, he suggests that we all ought to be insolent. As he sees it, "Any program which seeks to regularize the writing center's function is diametrically opposed to the very founding principles of the center. Our heritage, our lives place us on the fringe of the academy and to leave that fringe is to abandon who we are and what we do" (6). Further, he says, "Our function, our existence, our clients require us to be irregular, non-academic, firmly astraddle the boundary dividing academic culture from the rest of America" (6). Second, he suggests we be idealistic by realizing that "subverting the system . . . [is] well within our domain" (6). Finally, he recommends how we can be "creative," which appears to be a euphemism for "get by with little or nothing." Davis says, in fact, "We should get used to bad locations, inadequate resources, understaffing. We are academic slum dwellers, and we must accept the physical aspects of living there. If you take us out of the ghetto, you take the ghetto out of us" (7).

Though I've yet to find other articles that go to the depths of these two to articulate an iconoclastic position and though I can find many who argue with Riley and Davis (see, e.g., Grimm 1996b; Gardner and Ramsey 2005), the ideas contained in these two articles have been a refrain of the writing center story for decades. There is an ongoing tale that those working in writing centers ought to celebrate and guard their outsider positions and disdain the gold rings of the institutions where they are situated. I'm arguing that this sort of position is taken so frequently that there is pressure to conform to this narrative; storying writing center work as iconoclastic thus becomes part of the writing center grand narrative. Of course, like in every other chapter, there are consequences and counterstories to the grand narrative in the scholarship, notably Gardner and Ramsey's (2005) "The Polyvalent Mission of Writing Centers," which I'll get into later in this chapter. First, I want to examine how writing center professionals story the role or place of the writing center within their own institutions. After this, I'll show how writing center scholarship is also storied as iconoclastic or, at least, as "different."

ICONOCLASTIC SITES FOR LEARNING

There is little denying that writing centers in their various iterations are non-traditional when compared to the typical institutional approaches to education; writing centers often have no teachers, no lesson plans, no requirements for attendance, no credit, no schedule, no requirements for what should be taught, and no grades. Being non-traditional, however, requires an articulation of the relationship to the "traditional." If the writing center does not fit into the mold of education or teaching the rest of the university uses, how does it fit into the structure or institutional ecology? Over the years, many dozens of writing center professionals have weighed in on this question (see, e.g., Nicholas Mauriello, William Macauley, and Robert Koch's recent collection *Before and After the Tutorial* [Mauriello, Macauley, and Koch 2011] takes the writing center's institutional relationships as its starting point). For decades, scholars have worried that being non-traditional necessarily means *marginal*; no other word haunts writing center scholarship more than *marginal.*

Perhaps "marginal" weighs so heavily because if a writing center is marginal, the consequences are serious. For example, Virginia Perdue and Deborah James worry that marginal means invisible: "Because the teaching that occurs in writing centers is often informal, collaborative, and egalitarian, it is invisible. And this invisibility makes writing centers vulnerable to uncertain budgets, staffing, and locations, but most importantly, vulnerable to misunderstandings that marginalizes writing centers not just within our home institutions, but even within our departments' writing programs" (Perdue and James 1990, 7). This notion is also suggested by Stephen North and Lil Brannon, who suggest writing centers are feeder roots for the university or school system. They write: "Writing centers. . . nourish the plant system by transforming organic matter into nutrients that feed the system. They give the system stability. Yet feeder roots are not part of the world in the same way that the plant is: feeder roots remain underground, extending themselves into the earth, pushing always at the edges" (North and Brannon 2000, 10). Similarly, Christina Murphy and Joe Law worry that marginality means expendability: "The focus on remediation tended to push writing centers to the margins of the academy as a supplemental—essentially peripheral and expendable—instruction. Thus the first stage of writing center history was characterized both by this marginalization and by efforts to attain legitimacy within the academy" (Murphy and Law 1995, xi–xii). Marginality can also mean powerlessness. Marilyn Cooper worries that the marginality of writing center tutor status affects their ability to set or reset literacy agendas. She argues "because writing centers are marginalized in relation to the central institutional structures of writing pedagogy and writing center tutors are not generally expected to perform the function of intellectuals, the pressure on them to promulgate beliefs and practices that serve the purposes of the dominant group is less organized and less direct, although it is certainly not absent" (Cooper 1994, 344).

For these reasons—and others articulated over the decades—marginality is a loaded word for writing center professionals. Though the term appears so frequently in writing center scholarship it could be a trope—part of the writing center grand narrative—writing centers are rarely, simply called marginal in the way they are called "cozy," for example. Marginal is a deeply contested term; most writing center professionals would not embrace the term, although a few do. I'm arguing that in a very conscious effort to cast off the "marginal" story and its consequences, writing center scholars have restoried the writing center as iconoclastic. In other words, the "writing center as marginal" is so ardently rejected, the rejection has become part of the grand narrative. Gardner and Ramsey (2005) take a similar position when they assert that the writing center grand narrative is resistance. In the introduction to *Landmark Essays on Writing Centers,* the editors state that "the concerns of the original writing center movement are not lost, only modified by changing actualities. Writing center professionals still seek to explain and validate their work; they still battle to avoid marginalization and misapplication or writing center resources to non-compelling ends" (Murphy and Law 1995, xv). The "battle" to avoid actual marginalization or the label/story marginal is still with us. Further, the fact that the edited collection *Marginal Words, Marginal Works: Tutoring the Academy in the Work of Writing Centers* was published just a few years ago says something about the ongoing significance of the term. Therefore, for me, the strand of the writing center grand narrative is not the idea that a writing center is marginal (that isn't an identity claimed by most) but rather the persistent tendency of writing center professionals to re-story the marginal label into something else.

We can see elsewhere three common ways in which "marginal" is re-storied.

Refusal: We Are Not Victims, We Are Not Marginal

One way that writing center scholars have dealt with the label "marginal," is to refuse to wear it. Joyce Kinkead laments what she calls "a celebration of marginality" that can manifest among writing center professionals (Kinkead 1996, 37). "Messages that focus on what is being done to us (e.g., limited space and funding)," she writes, "rather than what we do well, place centers in a reactive rather than proactive stance" (37). She thinks the writing center community ought to have matured beyond a state of victimhood where others determine our image: "I am not suggesting that writing center personnel slather on silly happy faces, spout cheery thoughts, and ignore all negative reports like some kind of Stepford Staff. Rather, I suggest that our image is determined by us, and if the image we project is that of strong, capable, wise and caring teachers, then that is how we will be perceived" (37). Likewise, Jeanne Simpson writes, "I have come close to flaming on WCENTER over what sounds like pious victim-hood. It is NOT a blessed state. It is merely a common one. That we should attempt to make it less common is appropriate. We need not make it holy. For writing centers to fret about marginalization and/or victimization is to waste time. Define the specific problem and find a solution" (Simpson, Braye, and Boquet 1994, 156). Elsewhere, she denies the logic of the perceived marginalization of writing centers: "The concept of 'marginalization' would be a surprise to Central Administration. If a program is being funded, space provided, salaries paid, assessment and evaluation being conducted, then the assumption of Central Administration is that it is part of the institution and that some part of the institution's mission is being addressed" (Simpson 1995a, 190).

End-Dating: We Used to Be Marginal

In recent scholarship, writing center scholars have made the rhetorical move of admitting writing centers were once marginal or have the possibility to be marginal now, but, oh, how things have changed. Muriel Harris has written "as we become more involved with other programs on our campus or in our community, we become more integrated into the foundation of our institution. We aren't going to be perceived as hanging out on some margin if our centers are built into structures and programs that are integral to the institution's structure" (Harris 2011, x). Likewise, Michael Pemberton sees writing centers as becoming central to institutional systems: "Instead of seeing ourselves as marginalized or out of the mainstream, we are now thinking of ourselves as colleagues and contributors to larger institutional initiatives, to collaboration built to distribute our knowledge, training, and resources to others" (Pemberton 2011, 255). Likewise, both Murphy and Hawkes (2010) and Isaacs (2011) see new types of writing centers—multiliteracy centers and centers for writing excellence specifically—as paths for writing centers to become even more central to their home institutions. These tactics are a way to leave behind the marginal label.

Subversion: We Can Use Marginality

Somewhere between refusal and end-dating lies subversion. In this re-storying strategy, writers flip marginality. A well-known article in this vein, Stephen North and Lil Brannon's "The Uses of Margins," turns the supposed marginalized status of writing centers into a positive. The authors suggest that writing center professionals "must claim their institutional space within the academy as well as their connectedness to the periphery, to the areas and spaces outside" (North and Brannon 2000, 12). They say it is crucial that the writing center community learn to use their status: "At the same time, working underground at the periphery allows the writing center the possibility to teach and learn in new ways. When no one outside of writing centers notices or cares, writing centers have created for themselves an enviable site where transformative work might actually be possible. So learning how to exploit the margins both to their institutional advantage and to their enviable teaching advantage is crucial to the future of writing centers" (10). Similarly in *Noise from the Writing Center*, Beth Boquet writes: "Rather than assuming that writing centers arise from the margins, exist on the margins, and are populated by the marginal, we might instead view writing center staff and students as bastardizing the work of the institution. That is, we might say that they are not a threat from without but are rather a threat from within. We might seize the designation of institutional illegitimacy as a way of explaining our lack of faithfulness to our origins" (Boquet 2002, 32). In *Facing the Center*, Harry Denny echoes this sentiment. He describes his ideal center as "one whose accommodationist profile is leveraged for subversive work. It serves as a space for social and institutional changes that doesn't necessarily or directly benefit corporatist academic interests" (Denny 2010, 153). Likewise, in the introduction to *Marginal Words, Marginal Work?*, editors Bill Macauley and Nick Mauriello say they "never have strayed far from our shared sense of liking the margins" (Macauley and Mauriello 2007b, xiv). Either by "exploiting," "bastardizing," "subverting," or "liking" the margins these authors are still keeping writing centers on the outside looking in, albeit with a thumb to the nose.

This last strategy seems the most iconoclastic. The sense that writing centers are post-marginal, that they have matured out of a state of victimhood and neglect, as evidenced by the fact that they have persevered now seems to dominate. Yet, the marginal story was not replaced with a "mainstream" story. Writing center professionals still see their writing centers as outside the institutional mainstream. Now, though, the sense is that writing centers *want* to be outside it, because, as Davis and Riley rallied, that is where they belong. So why this story? Why are writing centers persistently written, as Mendelsohn says, "in but not of academic institutions" (Mendelsohn 2011, 90)? The payoff seems to be, regardless of the re-storying strategy, a way to overcome feelings of isolation and inferiority, a way to insist upon belonging even if that belonging looks different than more "traditional" or established campus entities. However, all of the reaction to the "marginal" label brings to mind George Lakoff's (2005) book *Don't Think of an Elephant.* Lakoff suggests that when someone tells you not to think about something, say an elephant, that is what you immediately do think of. Talking about not being marginal means talking about being marginal.

NON-TRADITIONAL SCHOLARSHIP, NON-TRADITIONAL SCHOLARS

The sense of writing centers being anti-institutional or anti-traditional manifests in the scholarship on writing centers, too. Perhaps less militantly than the ideological positioning of centers demonstrated by Davis or Riley, the iconoclastic nature of writing center research can perhaps best be summed up by Muriel Harris: "scholarship in this area looks different" (Harris 1997, 88). Though this difference is articulated by scholars in different ways, for Harris the difference is in the product of theorizing. Harris argues that writing centers themselves—not just publications—are the product of writing center scholarship:

> Like textbooks that contextualize and operationalize composition theory, every writing center is itself an application of theory to reality, an instantiation of theory. Setting up and running a writing center, like writing a textbook or structuring a composition curriculum, requires knowledge of a rather forbiddingly long list of matters that must be considered: the students to be served; the types of tutorial help they will need; instructional materials that will be needed; approaches that will be used to select, train, and evaluate tutors; faculty development needed for appropriate use of the writing center; the placement of the center within the institution and its mission; and administrative matters such as budget, space, public relations, paperwork, and assessment. (Harris 1997, 92)

Thus, she implies, while writing center professionals may not publish as a primary sign of their scholarly work, they will manifest their theoretical work in a functional and reflexive writing center design and in the institutional research directors must do and report. Harris (1999) addresses this issue in "Diverse Research Methodologies at Work for Diverse Audiences: Shaping the Writing Center to the Institution."

Likewise, Peter Carino in "Theorizing the Writing Center: An Uneasy Task" also writes about writing center scholarship. Here he explores the dichotomy of practice and theory, noting that writing centers historically have seemed to be aligned more closely with the former and skeptical of the latter (Carino 1995b, 124). He describes the push toward theory as "a means of establishing disciplinary and institutional respectability" (125), because "people who 'do' theory earn scholarly respect" (125). Yet, he reminds us of the difficulty of this undertaking for "facilities often underfunded and run by people with less than faculty status" (133). As illustration of this, he points to the 1980s when many in the field of composition were conducting empirical research on cognition and composition: "Although in the 1980s cognitive rhetoricians were conducting what they perceived as empirical research and calling for more, the writing center community ignored the call. This silence can be attributed partly to the institutional and professional politics that marginalized many center directors; struggling to keep their enterprises afloat and often denied full faculty status, few directors had time for the kind of research a cognitive theory of practice would require" (127). Thus, Carino would agree that writing center scholarship is different and points to one reason why: the institutional status of writing center professionals is often tenuous.

In "Writing as Social Process: A Theoretical Foundation for Writing Centers?" Lisa Ede writes about her experience of running a writing center and not being able to theorize her work. She writes: "I have come to believe that my situation is not uncommon. For a variety of reasons, those of us who direct or work in writing centers have seldom been able to articulate theoretical support for our work that goes beyond the basic principles of collaborative learning. The most common reason for this failure, of course, is that we have been too busy working ourselves to death—running centers on inadequate or even nonexistent budgets, functioning as director, secretary, tutor, and public relations expert all at once—to take time to theorize" (Ede 1989, 100). She notes that this made her feel like her theory self and writing center self were divided (100). Her article marks a rallying cry for the unification of her writing center self and theorizing self—a move she thinks will change the perception of writing centers. She says that "as long as thinking and writing are regarded as inherently individual, solitary activities, writing centers can never be viewed as anything more than pedagogical fix-it shops to help those who, for whatever reason, are unable to think and write on their own. This understanding of thinking and writing not only places writing centers on the periphery of most colleges, where our second-class status is symbolized by our basement offices and inadequate staffs and budgets, it also places us on the periphery of our own field of composition studies" (102). Acknowledging the difficulty of finding time for theorizing when there is so much doing to be done, Ede simply exhorts us to "fight for the time we need to do such thinking and writing" (106).

Ede's article reminds me of a moment at the International Writing Center Association Summer Institute a few years ago. About midway through the week-long intensive workshop, a writing center director stood up and said something to the effect of, "I appreciate how all the leaders are encouraging us towards informed practices grounded in research, but I don't have the time to read up on past research or stay current with what is coming out now." Many other participants nodded and voiced similar sentiments. The topic passed, yet later that afternoon one of the leaders stood up and took the group back to that earlier point saying, like Ede had in the article, "Your job is to make the time."

Likewise, a similar response can be found in one of the most damning passages of Harry Denny's *Facing the Center*:

> As Michele Eodice (2009), a former president of the International Writing Center Association, posed, would physics allow someone to pop up in a professional conversation and ask how to "do" being in the profession? Yet this sort of learning on the job is quite common in writing centers in spite of many arenas and outlets where people can receive professional training and education. What does that tell us about the state of our profession? Too often, we lack the intellectual curiosity or capacity to reflect on and understand what we do, why we do it, and under what contexts our moves work and don't work. To often, we turn to the larger community and want quick and dirty recipes for what to do in a pinch. Instead, we need to acknowledge that beyond the received wisdom is a history and corpus of scholarship that needs to be engaged, riffed on, and reinvigorated with our own lived experiments, observations, and critical interrogation. We need to, more directly, infuse our everyday practices with the currency of academic life: intellectual questioning and theorizing of what's possible. Otherwise, the profession continues on the margin, not by design, by as an effect. (Denny 2010, 146)

What Carino, Ede, the summer institute leader, and Denny all illustrate is how writing center scholarship is different; it may be both "undertheorized" when written—what Stephen North (1987) calls "lore"—and underutilized when published. In other words, there is too little scholarship and too little engagement in the scholarship. Eric Hobson suggests this is not an issue of laziness or naïveté but about epistemological preferences. He says the writing center community sees lore "as a valid (philosophically and methodologically) means of making knowledge" even though "we feel guilty about being more interested in the practice of writing center work than in its theory" (Hobson 1994, 2). Writing center professionals, Hobson suggests, see lore—like the conversations on WCENTER—as knowledge. But, since we feel like we should draw on theory over practice, writing center professionals have been looking for some "metatheory" to guide practice, an enterprise he finds lacking any hope. In the end, Hobson does not think we need to turn away from our preferences for lore but would rather scholarship engage practice as a way to make lore "count" (Hobson 1994, 9).[1]

Signs of the difference of writing center scholarship also manifest in the conferences associated with the field. A major difference of writing center conferences is that the audience and authorship of research includes both professionals and students. For instance, unlike writing studies at large, regional writing center conferences are plentiful and popular, especially for peer tutors. Undergraduate and graduate students are frequent—and if my region is any indication—often the majority of attendees and presenters at regional writing center conferences. By comparison, it is rare to find undergraduates, in particular, in attendance or presenting, say, at the Conference on College Composition and Communication.[2]

In addition, it is not just the conference attendees and presenters that are different. It is also conference formats. The 2012 International Writing Center Association Collaborative, for example, called itself an "unconference" and asked for proposals in a variety of unconventional formats including laboratories, collaborative writing circles, round-robin discussions, and fishbowl conversations. These formats may preclude a "presenter" all together, instead having guided conversations where the audience members in essence all become presenters; the focus is on talking and listening to one another and not on hearing someone's research. Many writing center conferences I've attended in the last decade have encouraged non-traditional formats and/or have insisted on audience involvement in more traditional panel presentations.

It is in Carino's call for the use of lore, the inclusion of students as researchers, and in the "unconference" conferences where I see writing center professionals reveal the way in which writing center professionals

---

1. Related to this is the popularity for Stephen North's (1984) "The Idea of a Writing Center" over his article "Writing Center Research: Testing Our Assumptions" as clearly articulated by Beth Boquet and Neal Lerner's (2008) "After 'The Idea of the Writing Center.'"

2. Students have publishing opportunities in the discipline, too. *Writing Center Journal* has just released an entire issue written by peer tutors (Fall 2012) and tutors are published in each issue of the *Writing Lab Newsletter* in the "Tutor's Column" and elsewhere.

story their scholarship as non-traditional and enact on the vision provided by that story. In Kris Fleckenstein's (2010) terms, they have rhetorical habits in which they value lore and practice perhaps at the cost of theory and research. They have conceptions of their scholarship as different—so different that it might not result in a publication but rather in the way the center functions or might well be written up in internal reports.[3] These rhetorical habits are entwined with visual habits that instruct members of this community to see scholarship in particular ways. That members of this community might *look for* scholarship that is implementable, practical, or easy to read might be because the rhetorical habits—the conventional way of writing about scholarship—has conditioned them to do so.

AT STAKE: CONSEQUENCES

The consequences of the story of writing centers and writing center scholarship as iconoclastic are real: this story influences one of the largest systemic issues in writing center studies—the rarity of tenure-track writing center director positions. If writing centers are outside of institutional structures and do not conduct scholarship recognized by academe, it follows that writing center directorships will not be tenure-track faculty positions. Some argue that directors need not be tenure-track faculty for job security or power, but, by and large, tenure-track faculty (must) produce research-based scholarship, can write writing center studies into courses and curriculums, and can serve on committees for theses and dissertations on writing centers. Many graduate students in rhetoric and composition are still being told not to focus theses and dissertations on writing centers because there is no one on faculty to advise. Of course, in the early days of composition, when composition was emerging as a field of study, there were few graduate programs that offered specialization in rhetoric and composition. English departments didn't graduate or hire composition specialists, so there was no question of tenuring those who taught composition. There were few journals that accepted "pedagogy" pieces on teaching writing, yet even if one did publish on the subject, it was not something that typically aided a tenure dossier. However, times have changed for scholars in rhetoric and composition. In fact, in the 1970s and 1980s, when compositionists started, essentially, an equal rights movement, writing center professionals joined in by crafting a number of position statements and

---

3. In Jackson and Grutsch McKinney (2011), we find that far more writing center directors report writing internal reports than they report doing scholarship.

resolutions that affirmed their desire to be seen as universal professionals. During this time, it seemed possible that another story of writing center professionals might emerge.

The first of the professional statements was the 1981 College Conference on Communication and composition (CCCC) resolution proposed by Mildred Steele, who describes the process of its passing in "Professional Status for Writing Center Directors." Here, she tells of attending an earlier CCCC in 1979 where a similar statement was written for composition faculty. When at that meeting, Steele suggested adding "and/or writing lab directors" into the document, the idea was "immediately challenged" (Steele 2002, 60). When introducing the 1981 proposal, professionalization was on her mind. Steele said, "To grow professionally, [writing center directors] need opportunities for scholarly reading, thought, and research. They need opportunities to work for advanced degrees. They should be able to travel to conferences to learn and to make presentations and to become informed of new approaches in language, rhetoric, and the teaching of writing in order to work compatibly with English faculty and others" (61). The resolution states:

> Whereas full-time professionals holding advanced degrees are widely employed by institutions of higher education to provide individualized instruction in writing labs;
>
> Whereas these writing lab professionals are not always accorded faculty status by their institutions and, hence, are subject to inequities in workload, in remuneration, and in career protection:
>
> Therefore, be it resolved that the 1981 CCCC affirm that full-time writing lab professionals holding advanced degrees, under contract to institutions of higher education, be accorded the same rights—equitable workloads, remuneration, and access to tenure—as other faculty members. (61)

In brief, this resolution said if or when a "professional" writing center director was hired, he or she should "be accorded the same rights" as other faculty. By 1981, the resolution was approved unanimously.

The second statement, passed a few years later by the National Writing Center Association (NWCA) in 1985, was similar in demands. The "Statement on Professional Concerns of Writing Center Directors" remains the only general statement on the professional status of WCDs to come from the NWCA, or what is now known as the International Writing Center Association (IWCA). According to author Jeanne Simpson, the position statement laid out an ideal that was likely rarely seen in actual settings; she writes that "most of us are unlikely to encounter working conditions as ideal as those suggested by the position statement" (Simpson 1995b, 36). The statement, which was quite extensive, states unequivocally an opposition to the hiring of part-time, temporary, unqualified, or underprepared writing center directors. The statement also recommends that "directorships should be considered faculty and administrative positions rather than staff positions" and "directorships should include access to promotion, salary, tenure, and travel funds equivalent to that provided for other faculty and administrators" (36). Further, the statement noted that writing center directors need preparation that includes teaching composition and coursework in theories of learning and research methods.

That same year, a survey in *The Writing Lab Newsletter* spoke to the situation of writing center director status. Of the 298 *Writing Lab Newsletter* subscribers who responded to the survey, just 26 percent were tenure or tenure-track. The majority, 55 percent, were in non-tenureable positions and the other 19 percent were in staff positions (Murray and Bannister 1985, 10). The 1985 NWCA position statement wanted to move directors out of the 55 percent column and into the 26 percent column. Two other related resolutions came in the decade following the NWCA position statement that also articulated a vision for professionalized compositionists. The Wyoming Resolution, which came about at CCCC in 1987, stated that "the salaries and working conditions of post-secondary teachers with primary responsibility for the teaching of writing are fundamentally unfair as judged by any reasonable professional standards (e.g., unfair in excessive teaching loads, unreasonably large class sizes, salary inequities, lack of benefits and professional status, and barriers to professional advancement)" (Robertson, Crowley, and Lentricchia 1987, 276).

Then, a few years later, the CCCC executive committee accepted the Portland Resolution (1992), which addressed the inequities of writing program administrator positions. Point 3 of the resolution reads:

> Job security. WPA positions should carry sufficient stability and continuity to allow for the development of sound educational programs and planning. The WPA should be a regular, full-time, tenured faculty member or a full-time administrator with a recognizable title that delineates the scope of the position (e.g., Director of Writing, Coordinator of Composition, Division or Department Chair). WPAs should have travel funds equivalent to those provided for other faculty and administrators and should receive a salary commensurate with their considerable responsibilities and workload (including summer stipends). Requirements for retention, promotion, and tenure

should be clearly defined and should consider the unique administrative demands of the position. (Hult et al. 1992, 90)

Though writing center directors are sometimes considered WPAs, this position statement clearly was intended to address only the inequities of WPAs who directed writing programs. Writing centers are mentioned just twice in this document (though the document itself shares much of the structure and language of the NWCA position statement): first when stating that "WPAs should have ample opportunities and release time to work in close consultation with colleagues in related fields and departments" (90), writing center directors are the first colleague listed. Second, when describing the WPA responsibilities, the Portland Resolution notes in parentheses "managing writing center staff" with an asterisk indicating "may be a separate position" (91). Because this statement only cursorily mentions writing centers, it has never been a point of much discussion for writing center professionals.

Still, the accumulation of these statements tells the extent to which teaching composition, directing writing centers, and directing writing programs was precarious work in the 1980s and 1990s. Composition was the sad step-sister of English departments and the collective action of many within the field aimed to end the untenability of many positions and the overall lack of respect. In "Polylog: Are Writing Center Directors Writing Program Administrators?" Melissa Ianetta et al. describe three different models of writing center director identities: administrative iconoclasts, local professionals, and universal professionals. The administrative iconoclast believes "writing program administrators are not only not part of Composition Studies, but that they shouldn't want to be—for such specialization is just another effete, pedigreed discourse that devalues the individualism at the foundation of ethical writing instruction. By extension, the ethical WPA (including the WCD) should avoid disciplinarity to resist the normalizing forces of the punishment-and-reward system of modern universities, where prestige—the badge of which is tenure—is most often attached to traditional notions of research and group instruction, not service and individualized instruction" (Ianetta et al. 2006, 16). Further, the administrative iconoclast does not have, need, or want a PhD, tenure, publications, or any other marker of institutional status. The local professional "assumes that WCDs should understand the best practices circulating in the field, but more importantly, they should have the professional ability to understand their individual contexts" (15). The universal professional holds "credentials clearly recognized in the academic universe, that is Composition Ph.D.s with relevant coursework, experience and mentoring in administrative matters" (14). The professional statements and professionalization movement was conscious effort to move writing center directorships from "administrative iconoclasts" to "universal professionals." Yet, this did not manifest.

After the acceptance of these position statements, a number of studies sought to see how well the benchmarks set in the statements were being met. In 1995, we get our first major survey of writing center directors from Dave Healy. His first sentence is perhaps revealing of the state of affairs: "Although writing centers have become institutionalized within the academy, their ubiquity has not resulted in anything approaching security among writing center personnel" (Healy 1995, 26). Among those who respond, he finds that "nearly all directors (96%) have a graduate degree: 44 percent with an MA, 40 percent with a PhD, and 12 percent with another degree (e.g., MEd, EdD, MFA). Writing center directors are most likely to be trained in English/literature (66%), followed by education (20%) and composition/rhetoric (10%) (Healy 1995, 30). Sixty-nine percent of those surveyed are faculty and 46 percent are tenure-track (30), though Healy notes that his sample skews to those in full-time positions since he sent surveys only to those who had joined NWCA or subscribed to the *Writing Lab Newsletter*. Valerie Balester and James McDonald (2001) surveyed writing center directors in 1997, and they found only 25 percent were tenure-line faculty in comparison with 77 percent of writing program administrators who were tenure-line faculty.

In 2001, the Writing Center Research Project began surveying WCDs every couple of years and includes questions related to status. They have not made public all of their survey data (unfortunately), but from the 2001 and 2003 survey, we have the numbers on what type of position directors are in. There is not much shift from Healy's 1995 survey; in 1995, Healy reported 46 percent were tenure-line. The WCRP reported 43 percent were tenure-line in 2001 and 41 percent were tenure-line in 2003 (see Table 4.1).

The most recent survey on the professionalization of writing center directors did not ask about tenure status, but did ask about specialization. Of 226 CWPA members surveyed by Jonnika Charlton (2009), 25 percent had a graduate specialization in rhetoric and composition, 50 percent had a specialty in literature, and the other 25 percent had indicated "other."

Table 4.1. Status of WCDs

Murray and Bannister (1985)

Tenured/tenure-track: 26%

Non tenure-track faculty: 55%

Not faculty: 19%

Healy (1995)

Tenured/tenure-track: 46%

Non tenure-track faculty: 23%

Not faculty: 31%

Balester and McDonald 1997 Survey (Balester & McDonald 2001)

Tenured/tenure-track: 25%

Non tenure-track faculty: 35%

Not faculty: 40%

WCRP (2001–2002)

Tenured/tenure track: 42%

Non tenure-track faculty full time: 21%

Non tenure-track faculty part time: 3%

Not faculty: 33%

Grad students: 1%

WCRP (2003–2004)

Tenured/tenure track: 41%

Non tenure-track faculty full time: 21%

Non tenure-track faculty part time: 3%

Not faculty: 34%

Grad students: 0.6%

Charlton's 2007 Survey (Charlton 2009)

WCD with graduate specialization in rhetoric and composition: 25%

WCD with graduate specialization in literature: 50%

WCD with other specialization: 25%

On a related note, far too few directors are permitted to teach graduate courses, design courses for the curriculum, or serve/direct graduate student projects. Sue Doe suggests that tenure is related to influence on curriculum. She writes, "The ability of writing centers to command institutional authority and demonstrate autonomy in curriculum, policy, and research decision-making is arguably jeopardized by the absence of tenure among many directors" (Doe 2011, 37). In real terms, this means that hundreds of writing center directors begin with no graduate course work in writing center or writing program administration. Very few graduate courses are consistently taught in writing center theory or administration, even today (Pemberton 2011). At most schools with graduate programs, only tenured or tenure-track faculty would be permitted to do so.

Not everyone would agree that whether or not one has a tenure-line matters to the work of a center or director. Neal Lerner, for one, has written that "professional status as equated with institutional security and leverage can come in many forms in many different contexts. A writing center director who is in a full-time staff position can be just as influential in an institution as can a tenured faculty member (or both can be equally lacking in influence)" (Lerner 2000, 44). When he wonders if we've become an unhappy professional landscape of "part-time or staff writing center directors coupled with an overworked tenure-track group" (36), I concede that tenure-line status is not the only marker of institutional privilege or general well-being. I know competent, smart, and successful writing center directors who are in contingent or secure staff positions (Neal Lerner calls the former the "have nots") who have taught me and pushed me to think about my writing center work in more critical ways. However, I know of many other writing center directors who find themselves in their positions with no background in teaching writing, no graduate coursework in composition studies, no awareness of scholarship on writing center theories or practice, and who remain unconnected to regional, national, and international writing center organizations. Denny says these folks are "doing time" in writing centers: "They clock in and out, they may have marginal training, an expertise in the field's scholarship, they may be effective, but just don't engage" (Denny 2010, 154). I know directors who are appointed to one-year and two-year positions, who are asked to teach too many classes or, alternatively, without faculty status are never on level-ground with their "academic" colleagues. In short, they are not professionalized and their appointments do not require or even allow them to be. For this group of directors, the dominant story of writing center director as iconoclastic—who doesn't need or want institutional markers of professionalization—is a story that may be personally satisfying but has pretty dire consequences for writing center studies. It seems no coincidence that the iconoclast anthems—Davis (1995) and Riley (1994)—came to the scene just as these professionalization efforts dropped off. We live the story we tell.

Today, "universal professional" writing center directorships are still hard to find (see Doe 2011; Nelson and Garner 2011). Melissa Nicolas began her article "Where the Women Are: Writing Centers and the

Academic Hierarchy," joking, "Recently, I have been out on the job market, hoping to secure a tenure track position as an assistant professor and writing center director with adequate release time to run the writing center and conduct my research at an institution that will value my writing center work as an administrator and researcher as something more than a mere committee assignment. I know. I know. Many of you have fallen off your chairs laughing by now" (Nicolas 2004, 11). She recounts hiring committees questioning her motives for wanting to direct a center: "I specifically recall one campus visit where I had to convince the search committee that writing center work was my first choice and that I was not some literature scholar in disguise, taking a writing center job until something 'better' came along. This visit ended with the department chair assuring me that if I took the director position, I would not have to stay in the writing center permanently, that I could move out of the center and, I guess, up a rung or two on the ladder of institutional respect" (Nicolas 2004, 11). I remember a similar reaction when I took a tenure-track position as a writing center director and a member of my dissertation committee said, "A lot of good people start out in writing centers," a signal to me that writing centers were not a place to stay. Thus, even those transgressing the iconoclast identity in departments who think enough of writing center work to hire a scholar to direct the center may still find the iconoclast stigma very sticky. Nicolas (2004, 2007) blames the feminization of the writing center narrative for the continual degradation of writing centers, and I do think that she's onto something, but I also think writing center professionals themselves play a role with their continuous propagation of the iconoclast story irrespective of gender politics.

PERIPHERAL VISIONS

A grand narrative seems totalizing, but never is. There are alternative voices to the iconoclast story, even if they are peripheral. Most notably, Gardner and Ramsey deconstruct the marginal/not marginal, inside/outside, regulation/emancipation binaries that haunt writing center scholarship. They simply say that "marginality has neared the end of its usefulness" (Gardner and Ramsey 2005, 26) and encourage readers to see that writing centers and the institutions they are found in are always both—marginal and not marginal, emancipatory and regulatory. Likewise, Mendelsohn wonders about the usefulness of the insider/outsider binary: "Yet this reconceptualized writing center topography, in which institutional liminality is rewritten as a virtue rather than a limitation, can be an equally restrictive conceptual model. If writing centers' status as separate and between is consistently understood as a strength, how might that limit administrators' ability to recognize the potential benefits of certain institutional partnerships? In other words, what happens when liminal centers become joiners? What happens when centers—to meet the needs of writers, to thrive—form partnerships that demand participation in another academic culture?" (Mendelsohn 2011, 90). Thus, Mendelsohn, too, pushes us to see how writing centers are already enmeshed in university ecologies despite the story we tell. Nonetheless, like a pony ride at the zoo, we keep circling back to the same paths. Even as Gardner and Ramsey (2005) and Mendelsohn (2011) want to move us away, we have to plod over familiar territory once again. In order to say the iconoclastic story has consequences, we have to rehash the iconoclastic story. Part of the problem is certainly the tendency to think about it in binaries. If we are not iconoclasts, then are we The Man?

We've been too narrowly focused on one question: what is or what should be the writing center's status in the university? The focus on that question has given us tunnel vision; it encourages an endless march toward progress. The answer is often couched in an apology or a defensive posturing for not being more. Here's the truth: a writing center can be effective in any size or configuration. A writing center is exactly as big and as influential as the ecology allows it to be. The status of a center is an existential question on par with "Who am I?" and "Why am I on this earth?" It is both unanswerable and infinitely answerable. But it is not so curious that writing center professionals keep returning to the same answer when we remember what Jerome Bruner has written about how we come to (life) stories: "Given their constructed nature and their dependence upon the cultural conventions and language usage, life narratives obviously reflect the prevailing theories about 'possible lives' that are part of one's culture. Indeed, one important way of characterizing a culture is by the narrative models it makes available for describing the course of a life. And the tool kit of any culture is replete not only with a stock of canonical life narratives (heroes, Marthas, tricksters, etc.), but with combinable formal constituents from which its members can construct their own life narratives: canonical stances and circumstances, as it were" (Bruner 2004, 694). In other words, our culture(s) provides us with genres, characters, conventions—what Fleckenstein (2010) would call rhetorical habits—for telling our stories. These habits become so entrenched that they "become recipes for structuring experience itself" (Bruner 2004, 708).

In other words, we're stuck on the pony ride.

Until we ask other questions that widen our purview and we come back to the material realities of our centers, scholarship, and positions. Bruner also tells us that any story is just a representation. If we put aside our rhetorical and visual habits that have us continually wrapped in discussing and seeing ourselves as marginal or not marginal, we might see other perfectly viable, perhaps even more useful representation.

5

WRITING CENTERS TUTOR (ALL STUDENTS)

We not only produce our identities through the practices we engage in, but we also define ourselves through the practices we do not engage in. Our identities are constituted not only by what we are but also by what we are not. To the extent that we can come in contact with other ways of being, what we are not can even become a large part of how we define ourselves.

—Etienne Wenger (1999), *Communities of Practice*

Some years ago at the writing center I was directing, we offered instant messaging (IM). This was before Facebook had chatting capabilities and before unlimited texting plans, so many undergraduate students used IM as a primary means for communication with their peers. We had our IM box embedded into the home page of our website, and we invited students—or whoever was on the page—to ask us "quick questions" there. For a couple of years, this was a popular way for us to communicate with students; far more students IMed us than called or emailed us. Because of the popularity, I studied the tutor and student interactions via IM, wrote my findings up, and presented them at a writing center conference. Before my presentation during lunch at that conference, the conversation at my table, as it often does at conferences, turned toward what everyone was presenting on. When it was my turn, I talked about what my center had been doing with IM and what I found from studying the IM use and transcripts. The reaction from the table was one of resistant curiosity. Person A asked, "Aren't you worried that tutors would just be giving answers to students' questions?" and "Shouldn't the students just make appointments?" Person B asked, "Are you sure that only students from your school are using the chat box?" And Person C said, "That sounds interesting, but our center focuses on *tutoring.*" This conversation helped me reframe my presentation that night in my hotel room as I then knew the dimensions of the counterarguments to my claims, but more importantly here, it helped me to see the perimeters writing center professionals have put on the work of the writing center:

writing center work, we're told, is about tutoring students—and a particular breed of tutoring that takes place in one-to-one sessions of a designated length and of a particular pedagogy that is more about conversation than answers.

This chapter takes under consideration the main clause of the writing center grand narrative that writing centers are *places where all students go to get one-to-one tutoring on their writing*. As such, I'm asking that we pause to think about that idea as a story, as one possible representation of writing center work among other possible representations, which might take a feat of imagination. Throughout the decades, it has become increasingly more challenging to imagine a writing center whose primary purpose, its raison d'être, is not one-to-one tutoring. No matter what differences we can point to from center to center, writing center professionals across the country believe that they have one-to-one peer tutoring in common if nothing else.[1] I don't think I'm going out on a limb to say that here, now, in the early twenty-first century, writing centers are typically places for individual tutoring on writing and that much of the theoretical discussions in writing center studies concerns pedagogies, approaches, and ideological implications of individualized writing instruction. Tutoring is the sine qua non of writing center work. A writing center is not a writing center without one-to-one tutoring.

In this chapter, I'll first point to scholarship that reinforces the story that tutoring is the work of a writing center as I have in previous chapters, but this chapter also includes empirical research. In a discipline like writing center studies, it hardly seems appropriate to insist on some "common" story based *only* on what is published in scholarly journals since so many writing center practitioners—like undergraduate peer tutors and contingent faculty administrators—participate less frequently in the field's publications. Thus, the discourse of writing centers exceeds official publications. To get a sense if the grand narrative also exceeds publication—if it is part of the larger discourse surrounding writing centers too—this chapter includes findings from a survey of those involved with writing center work.

SCHOLARSHIP

The story that writing centers are *places where all students go to get one-to-one tutoring on their writing* has its roots throughout writing center scholarship. Of all the parts of the narrative, the idea that writing centers

---

1.   There seems to be some consensus that international writing centers will often operate differently.

are places for one-to-one tutoring seems so commonsensical that it is implicit if not explicit in nearly every writing center publication. Nancy Grimm has written it "is seemingly one of the least controversial statements a person can make about writing centers" (Grimm 2011, 76). Tutoring is seen as the great connector; the single thing that all writing centers have in common, the *work* of a writing center. As such, I won't spend much time trying to prove that writing centers see tutoring as central to their work; I doubt there would be much objection to this point. Instead, I want to further clarify what tutoring means for writing centers. In Muriel Harris's "SLATE (Support for the Learning and Teaching of English) Statement: The Concept of A Writing Center," she writes, "Although writing centers may differ in size, specific services, source of staffing, and organizational procedures," they share in common approaches to tutoring. She delineates the six shared approaches across writing centers:

1. Tutorials are offered in a one-to-one setting.
2. Tutors are coaches and collaborators, not teachers.
3. Each student's individual needs are the focus of the tutorial.
4. Experimentation and practice are encouraged.
5. Writers work on writing from a variety of courses.
6. Writing centers are available for students at all levels of writing proficiency. (Harris 1988)

As such, for Harris, a writing center in the late 1980s might be many things, but it must be focused on tutoring to be a writing center. The descriptions of each of these shared approaches references tutoring even if the approach does not include the word "tutoring," "tutor," or "tutorial" (though most do). This SLATE statement has been posted in its entirety on the International Writing Center Association website (where it remains as recent as 2012 when I was revising this chapter), which speaks to its enduring importance and influence. Others echo Harris's sentiments. Diane George and Nancy Grimm have called one-to-one instruction the "primary responsibility" of a writing center (George and Grimm 1990, 62). Christina Murphy and Joe Law note "peer tutoring has been central to writing center pedagogy" (Murphy and Law 1995, xii).

More recently, Teddi Fishman describes the "cardinal rules of tutoring" for Clemson's Multiliteracy Studio, which seem to follow very closely from early writing center guides and Harris's concept. Fishman says tutors (what they call "associates") are trained to uphold these rules:

1. The focus of any session should be on the development of understanding and skills, rather than the development of a particular text.
2. Whatever the work is, it is the student's work.
3. The student should set the agenda.
4. Associates are not permitted to offer options about or assessments of grades.
5. Associates can neither interpret nor critique assignments. (Fishman 2010, 68–69)

Similarly, Grimm notes three "ubiquitous mottos" that writing centers rely on:

1. A good tutor makes the student do all the work.
2. The ultimate aim of a tutorial is an independent writer.
3. Our job is to produce better writers, not better writing. (Grimm 2011, 81)

She says these practices are rarely examined critically because "they have become our common sense" (81).

Further, it is not merely that tutoring is the main story of writing center work; writing center paradigms dictate a specific sort of tutoring as sources from Harris (1988) to Fishman (2010) to Grimm (2011) reveal. The tutoring is almost always assumed to be one-to-one, peer-to-peer, non-directive, and occurring in set sessions. "Tutoring" in writing center scholarship or training guides is not a catchall term like "teaching" is. "Teaching" can imply a range of activities, students, curriculums, and purposes. I can *teach* my six-year old to tie his shoes. I can also *teach* faculty on my campus how to respond to writing in a workshop. Or I can *teach* students to write reviews of literature in a college first-year writing course. On the contrary, "tutoring," for writing center professionals, means a very specific activity. So I'm suggesting that the writing center grand narrative defines writing center work very narrowly as tutoring, and I want to underscore that tutoring as conceptualized (and practiced) by many writing center professionals is also very narrow. For this reason, I came to realize that instant messaging rubbed some writing center professionals the wrong way because it violated many of these "norms"; it didn't look enough like tutoring, and tutoring must be the primary goal of a writing center. Instant messaging was spontaneous, it was anonymous, no papers were exchanged, tutors "just gave answers"— it was pretty directive, and it was public. It defied record-keeping.

The writing center–specific type of tutoring is promoted in a number of tutor training manuals. Though director resources exist (see. e.g.,

Murphy and Stay 2006), almost all manuals for working in a writing center are about tutoring. Further, the titles of the manuals reveal the type of tutoring assumed to happen in centers. Paula Gillespie and Neal Lerner's (2007) guide is called *The Longman Guide to Peer Tutoring*, which assumes tutors are peers or, minimally, that only the peer tutors need a training guide. It is not uncommon, in fact, for "peer tutoring" to be used as shorthand for "writing center tutoring." Moreover, Ben Rafoth's (2000) guide *A Tutor's Guide: Helping Writers One on One* and Muriel Harris's (1986) landmark book *Teaching One-to One: The Writing Conference* both assume writing center tutoring involves individualized instruction. In *The Everyday Writing Center*, Geller et al. suggest that these tutoring manuals might be responsible for tutoring "gospel," the specific type of tutoring promoted in writing centers (Geller et al. 2007, 21). They say, "Familiar memes—don't write on the paper, don't speak more than the student-writer, ask non-directive questions—get passed among cohorts of writing tutors as gospel before they even interact with writers" (21). Even if we all agree that tutoring should be *the* work of the writing center (which is a debatable point, I think), Geller et al. point out that it's only by choice that we all agree to tutor in the same way. I agree and would further suggest that writing centers do have some plurality in their tutoring practices but feel obliged to story it in a consistent way: *we are tutoring right*, they say.

SURVEY

As mentioned, to get a sense if what I've noticed as the writing center grand narrative takes place outside of writing center scholarship, I decided to survey members of the WCENTER and SSWC listservs about their ideas concerning writing centers. I wanted to see how writing center professionals and those working with writing centers story writing center work; do they write about tutoring and if so, do they share common visions? After receiving approval from the Institutional Review Board at my university, I posted a query to both listservs, asking for participants to complete the online survey (listserv members were also invited to send the query along to others) in April 2011. I also posted invitation links on Twitter and Facebook. I indicated that anyone associated with writing centers could participate, including those working *in* writing centers, those working *with* writing centers, and those *studying* writing centers. With the survey, I hoped I might hear from those involved in writing center work that might or might not be typically represented in writing center scholarship. And I did.[2]

---

2.   Though the readership to these listservs (especially WCENTER) is large and solic-

The survey contained eight questions: three multiple-choice questions and five open-ended questions. (I've included the results of the survey in the appendix because I've found the responses deeply engaging and want to offer readers a chance to find their own patterns along with the brief analysis I'm able to offer here.) One hundred seventeen people responded to the survey including administrators, faculty, professional staff, and undergraduate and graduate students from secondary schools, two-year colleges, and public and private four-year colleges.

To analyze the responses, I focused on four of the open-ended questions:

1. In your own words, what is a writing center?
2. How do you describe the role of your writing center to those at your own school?
3. In what ways do you think your writing center is different from other writing centers?
4. In what ways do you think your writing center is similar to other writing centers?

With these questions, I aimed to see how respondents thought about writing centers; in particular, I wanted to see how they storied writing centers and if the stories resembled the writing center grand narrative. I felt the four questions would help to show a respondent's specific and particular idea of a writing center and then also a more general idea of what a writing center is.

I've included the survey data in this chapter even though all three main clauses of the writing center grand narrative appear in the data—writing centers are cozy, writing centers are iconoclastic, and writing centers tutor all students—and the last of these is the most prominent. Specifically, respondents note that the writing center is a place, it is for all students, it is focused on one-to-one instruction, and the focus is tutoring.

What was most interesting in reading the survey results was seeing how tacit the writing center story is. Respondents expected I'd fill in the blanks. Ideas were so naturalized that they left things unsaid. (Or at least I'm guessing that they did.) Take for example, respondents who answered the question, "In your own words, what is a Writing

---

iting these groups is reliably the easiest way to reach hundreds of writing center scholars and practitioners in one email, the sample likely skews toward those more "professionalized"—those who know the listserv exists, have joined, and (probably) read WCENTER posts.

Center?," by saying, "A writing center is a place where students can go to improve their writing skills," "It's a friendly space where students can go to have a conversation about writing," or "A place where writers work together to help each other." From other answers by these same respondents, I can see that tutoring is a focus for each of these centers, but the word "tutoring" or "consulting" doesn't appear in their answers to the first question. All that these answers say is that a writing center is a place for help, for conversation, or for helping someone else. I think that the respondents assumed that the action of the center is implied, unnecessary to say. Needless to say, this made analysis a bit tricky, especially when I started by coding for keywords. Still, I was able to trace notable trends for each of the keywords in this part of the grand narrative: *writing centers are places where all students go to get one-to-one tutoring on their writing.*

PLACES

The clearest finding from the open-ended survey responses was that respondents described centers as a "place" (124 times), "space" (35 times), or "environment" (11 times). A vast majority of respondents used one of these terms in the first question (describe a writing center) and/or the second question (describe your writing center). Beth Boquet (1999) asks whether the writing center is a place or a method and the responses here indicate to me that respondents primarily conceive of centers as places (though they also will describe method). Notably, a few respondents also described the space as "safe," "comfortable," or "friendly," words that invoke the "writing centers as cozy" trope.

ALL STUDENTS

The sixth shared practice on Harris's (1988) list explains how centers work with students at all levels, and many respondents did report that their writing centers worked with all students. One writes, "I tell students and professors that the writing center helps students of all abilitie [*sic*] levels with writing in all subjects and disciplines and all aspects of the writing process." Another writes: "A process-focused writing environment where students can get help with every phase of a writing project from concept to mechanics. A 'no grade' zone in which students are met at their level of writing needed and boosted to the next level of accomplishment." The word "all" appears 104 times in the responses to the four open-ended questions analyzed here; albeit not every use is followed by "student." However, the words "student" and "students" are used a whooping 362 times in the responses. Students are indeed important in how respondents talk about writing centers. As a point of comparison, the words "faculty," "professors," and "teachers" appear much less frequently—only 81 times.

ONE-TO-ONE

Respondents noted that the work in their centers included one-to-one feedback. The terms "one-to-one" and "one-on-one" were used a total of twenty times. Moreover, the terms "individual" and "individualized" were used twenty-one times—often as adjectives modifying "sessions," "instruction," and "assistance." I was surprised that terms indicating individualized instruction was not used more, but as a point of comparison, there were only six responses that indicated group instruction as a primary function of writing centers.

TUTORING

As mentioned, tutoring seems implied in many of the answers, but it is also explicitly named frequently. The words "tutor," "tutors," "tutoring," and "tutorials" are used 186 times. Surprisingly, perhaps, the terms "consultant," "consulting," and "consultation" are used just 36 times. Many seem to assume that "consultant" is preferable to "tutor"; however, these findings suggest that tutor is still the dominant term. The words "help," "assistance," and "support" are also frequent—used a combined 166 times—illustrating perhaps the centers' favored position (a place for helping) in relation to students.

Beyond tutoring and helping, other writing center work is rarely mentioned. Workshops are noted just eleven times and the availability of resources indicated only fifteen times. As we'll see at the end of the chapter, these are near universal activities in writing centers yet rarely seen as such.

As I mentioned in the previous section, a specific type of tutoring is encouraged in some of the literature on writing centers. Since the survey questions did not directly address what approach to tutoring that respondents used, there were just a couple of descriptors for the method or approach to tutoring that surfaced as trends in the answers. The first was the focus on higher-order concerns (HOCs) over (or before) lower-order concerns (LOCs). For example, one wrote, "We try to work on higher order concerns before lower order concerns," as a way that the center was similar to others. The second idea about tutoring that came up a few times was distinction between tutoring and editing. One wrote,

"I describe [our writing center] as really helpful, not just an editing service, etc." And another wrote, "We do occasionally have to remind faculty that we're not an editing service." However, there were responses where editing was included as part of the mission, like in this one: "A place where any member of the community can come to get help with writing at any time during the process: planning, drafting, revising, editing, etc." Both of these ideas (HOCs and editing) seem to me to speak to the tacit understanding that writing center professionals engage in a particular type of tutoring.

Much more, of course, could be said about the responses from the survey beyond the keywords from the narrative that I was curious about here. For one, how respondents see their centers as similar or different to others is particularly interesting. Several noted their center was "different" because they had only professional or faculty tutors; yet other respondents said they were different because they had only peers. Others said they were different because they didn't have online tutoring, or one because they only had online tutoring. Some respondents thought they were better or worse funded than other centers, larger or smaller. Collectively, these responses can give the air of Goldilocks—a writing center is big, but not too big; funded, but not that well-funded; peer-based, but not just peers; online, but not just online. It seems a delicate walk to walk. Not a single respondent seemed to think their center was absolutely the epitome of writing centers everywhere. Thus, the answers in this survey do verify that what I've called the writing center grand narrative does show up in other discourse surrounding writing centers. Simultaneously, the survey results show that other stories are possible, if not yet dominant.

BENEFITS AND CONSEQUENCES

Describing writing center work as primarily involving tutoring writing does not seem, for me, and I suppose for others, like a rhetorical move. It seems as if I am just telling it as it is. But reading Jerome Bruner (2004), when he discusses how there is no "just as it is," that every representation leaves out something and necessarily emphasizes something else, makes me think harder about describing writing center work as tutoring. If we describe writing centers as primarily places for the tutoring of writing, we must get something for that telling. Stories do work, and a dominant story does not remain dominant if the work it does will not benefit the tellers in some way. So in what ways does this part of the writing center grand narrative benefit us?

Well, for starters, the idea of tutoring is legible, comprehensible. Saying we tutor will make sense to nearly everyone, inside and outside of the institution. Tutoring is not an obscure idea. So, as a way to say something quickly about the work of a writing center, it is easy to talk about tutoring. Of course, how we tutor might be different than outsiders anticipate, but the general concept makes sense. In fact, it is because of the legibility of the term that I prefer "tutoring" to the supposedly more egalitarian terms "consulting" or "coaching" or "mentoring." Regardless, whatever we call it, if we communicate that we have staffed folks who can give one-to-one writing feedback, the concept typically does not strike people as mysterious, superfluous, or cutesy. This works in our favor in terms of building allies and budgets. Nicholas Mauriello, William Macauley, and Robert Koch would agree on the legibility of the idea of tutoring. In "An Invitation to the 'Ongoing Conversation,'" they say campus communities understand very clearly what writing centers do: "For many others on campus—faculty, students, staff, and administrators—there is often a sound byte associated with writing centers: They tutor!" (Mauriello, Macauley, and Koch 2011, 1).

Tutoring also seems innocuous. The writing center is a support service, most believe, with no ambitions of being part of the curriculum. Students bring in the work they are completing for classes and tutors help them reach the goals that the instructors have set (or, at least, this is the common expectation). This is to say, naming our role as tutoring communicates that we are not trying to steer the ship but rather we'll work the oars, keeping things going in the direction the leaders have pointed us in (recall North and Brannon's 2000 metaphor of the feeder roots mentioned in the last chapter). Nancy Grimm explains, writing center professionals "are expected not to change what students learn but to get students to conform to institutional expectations and values" (Grimm 1996a, 530). Further, in the age of academic scarcity when all of our colleagues become possible competition for the ever-depleting pool of resources, saying we offer tutoring is a way to define our niche, to remove the threat of our presence as a curricular player, and to underscore our desire to help when others want to strip support, benefits, and comforts to which academics have become accustomed.

Focusing on tutoring makes another aspect of our work easier: counting. Though centers have increasingly spoken of a desire, named by Stephen North, to "make writing centers the centers of consciousness about writing on campus" (North 1984, 442), this is difficult to measure.

It is monumentally easier to put little tables of data in our annual reports listing how many students we tutored and how often. It is easy, if we are counting tutoring sessions, to compare one year to the next and to have quantitative data that speaks to our efficiencies and progress. In fact, non-tutoring work in a writing center seems to take hold in direct proportion to how countable it is. Similarly, many writing centers are asked to do an assessment of student learning goals (see, e.g., Hawthorne 2006). A focus on tutoring allows for the development of student learning outcomes that feed into assessment protocols. Counting does lead to pressure, however. Nicole Kraemer Munday writes, "In order to thrive, writing centers need to draw in writers" (Munday 2011, 105); likewise, Lisa Johnson-Shull and Diane Kelly-Riley assert the writing center's main goal is "to keep students coming in and coming back" (Johnson-Shull and Kelly-Riley 2001, 27). The logic, borrowed from the fast-food industry, is that if one thousand students served is good, two thousand students served is even better.

By telling the story of a writing center as a tutoring place, we represent ourselves, then, as important, helpful, yet not domineering. We seem virtuous and successful when we tally up each semester how many students we've helped. As I said in the introduction, this part of the grand narrative and what it connotes is desirable and, for whatever it matters, at least partly true. Writing centers *do* provide tutoring. But like all grand narratives, the story tries to be representative or universal but never succeeds. It is my argument in this book that telling the writing center grand narrative does have its benefits, but there are consequences particularly in what the story asks us to see and asks us to look past. The consequences of narrating a writing center first and foremost as a tutoring center are often overlooked as inevitable.

The first of these—one that is surely familiar to writing center professionals—is the sense that tutoring services, by their very nature, are remedial. The remedial label is so despised that students will avoid getting tutoring so as not to be seen as deficient, stupid, or ill-fit for academic work. Not just for students, the stigma of remedial labels was the cause of the closure of Dartmouth's Writing Clinic in 1960, according to Neal Lerner. The clinic, which opened in the late 1930s, closed its doors and directed students to tutors off-campus because university officials decided that writing remediation "does not seem a proper responsibility of a distinguished college" (Lerner 2007, 25). The Dartmouth College administrators and faculty felt the presence of a writing center marked the entire college as deficient.

Writing center professionals have for some time responded to the stench of remediation by making a concerted attempt to market and cater to all students—not just those who *need* help. Beth Boquet has said that "we fetishize the numbers of students we see from every end of campus" in efforts to prove we help everyone (Boquet 2002, 43). Recall that many survey respondents all indicated helping all students as part of their mission. Though this response is ardent and ongoing enough to be convincing among writing center professionals, many students and colleagues remained unconvinced. Perhaps this is because it is a rarity for students to seek additional help or simply discussion in a subject in which they are passing or in which they feel confident in their abilities. (Not to be mistaken, writing centers *do* work with students—perhaps even frequently—who are of high ability.)

It is worth pausing to think about whether it is really a *consequence* that a writing center be seen as remedial. What's wrong with remedial services after all? As Lerner suggests at the conclusion of his article, "Writing programs offer the possibility for higher education to represent the cultivation of intellect that is essential to our democratic ideals. While this might seem like a brand no longer in favor, that lofty purpose, particularly for students poorly served by their previous schooling, is a brand well worth reclaiming" (Lerner 2007, 31). Why not wave the remedial flag proudly? We know that students come to colleges with a wide-range of abilities and experiences with writing and we could champion those efforts. Though I agree that writing programs and writing centers have a responsibility to all students, the consequence of a remedial label is primarily perilousness. As the Dartmouth example suggests, being perceived as a service for students who do not meet university expectations upon entering can put the service on the chopping block when the university or college wants to assert a level of excellence or "standards." When I was a teaching assistant in my master's program, students who failed a diagnostic essay their first day at college were sent out of first-year composition and *down the road* to the local community college to take basic writing. The message was clear: you do not meet the expectations of this university and it is not our responsibility to remediate you.

A second consequence of the writing center being primarily conceived of as a tutoring center is related to remediation. This consequence is the unwitting participation in what David Coogan (1999, xv) calls "the strategy of containment." Instead of sending students down the road to another school as my former program did, many instructors simply send students to the writing center, thereby isolating the writing deficiencies in individual students and making the "problem" of difference an individual's concern, not an institutional one. Not infrequently, instructors drop off students at the front door of writing centers with a smile and the explanation, "She needs help." Mike Rose calls this sort of act "scholastic quarantine," where students sit "until their diseases can be diagnosed and remedied" (quoted in Lerner 2007, 17). In particular, the writing center emphasis on one-to-one tutoring encourages students to bear the responsibility for their (perceived) lack of preparedness. One by one students come to the writing center (in droves) to confess strikingly similar admissions of inadequacy conferred on them by instructor comments. Most telling are instructors who send entire classes to the center—"None of them know what they are doing!"—rather than coming to an equally viable conclusion that the instructor has not sufficiently taught them what to do.

Nancy Grimm writes of something similar in "The Regulatory Role of Writing Centers," where she asserts, "I am going to take an unhappy approach to writing center work and suggest that we don't always accomplish as much as we think we do and that in the long run we sometimes do more harm than good" (Grimm 1996b, 5). She notes the writing center's complicity in maintaining institutional goals (or barriers, depending how you look at it). Writing centers use one-to-one tutoring to "correct, measure, and supervise abnormal writers in order to meet the standards set by the institution" (7). Because, she writes, "Our culture teaches us to locate the problem of literacy in individuals and the solution in institutional practices" (8). Tutoring, and this is very important, keeps us focused on changing individual students. Think of the number of non-native speakers of English who come regularly to have their writing sound more "American." We work with these students; however, tutoring does nothing to change the climate on campus to move teachers toward greater acceptance of varied Englishes. Consequently, "Students perceive writing centers as places that help them get by rather than places where they can figure out how to change or challenge the system" (13). This again is something that makes us feel good—that students need us. But tutoring keeps us from asking why they need us; writing center work becomes about meeting needs and not about evaluating systems. It can feel like we keep bandaging up the war-wounded, fixing them up for their next battle without ever seeing if something can be done about the war.

More recently, in "Retheorizing Writing Center Work," Grimm takes this line of argument a step further. Grimm argues that "an ideology of individualism not only shapes writing center discourse but also races writing center practice, making it inhospitable to students who are not white" (Grimm 2011, 76). In other words, writing center practice—the act of one-to-one tutoring—is raced and potentially racist. Further, she notes that although most writing center professionals think they are simply being helpful, "Within this system, those of us who are white and/or middle class (no matter how well-intentioned and helpful) carry privilege" (79). Grimm takes umbrage with many of the so-called standard ways of tutoring in a writing center—focus on HOCs, Socratic questioning, reading aloud, indirect advice. As she says, "They ensure that white students will receive the assistance they need to improve their performance and that nonwhite students will encounter condescending assumptions and ineffectual practices" (84). To sum up, isolating the individual as the site of writing center education, yet insisting on universal tutoring practices (*every session should . . .*), for Grimm, is not only not helpful, it is possibly harmful to students.

What Grimm points to shows up elsewhere in our discourse, too. We say we want all students to come to our centers, to feel "comfortable" in our "non-traditional" setting, but when we narrate normal and abnormal tutoring scenarios in tutor training manuals, we reveal our unease with working with a vast array of students. This issue was raised about the subject positions of ESL students and students with learning disabilities by Jean Kiedaisch and Sue Dinitz in "Changing Notions of Difference in the Writing Center: The Possibilities of Universal Design." They note that it is nearly always assumed that a student, not a tutor, has a learning disability or is non-native when those topics are introduced (Kiedaisch and Dinitz 2007, 43).

In the tutor guides, patterns emerge that indicate other troubling assumptions about students, teachers, and tutors. Most interesting to me are the "types" of students or sessions that the authors of these guides draw attention to. The effect is to make me as a reader positioned to see these sort of students or sessions as abnormal—as not what we expected. *The Bedford Guide*, for example, discusses the writer who comes at the last minute (Ryan and Zimmerelli 2009, 99); the unresponsive writer (100); the antagonistic writer (101); the writer with an inappropriate topic or offensive language (102); the writer who plagiarizes (102); the writer with the perfect paper (105); and the writer with the long paper (105). *The Longman Guide* gives advice on what to do when the writer is crying (Gillespie and Lerner 2007, 161); won't revise (162); won't listen (162); is dependent (162); is tutor surfing (163); is not cooperating (163); frightens you (164); has chosen a really bad topic (165); is emotionally invested and can't write paper (166); has a paper full of errors (167); can't recognize errors (167); has far to go (167); and won't quit (167). Ironically, the only "issue" the tutor might have, according to the *Longman Guide* or *What the Writing Tutor Needs to Know*, is that he or she might care too much and thus talk too much.

On the more disturbing side, many of the guides caution that tutors might have to work with students who are "different" in their learning style, writing level, first language, learning (dis)abilities, age, nationality, race (or "multiculturalism"), dialect, or gender. One guide, almost comically, tells the tutor he or she will work with different students, but "you will be happy to know that there is no need to develop a new approach to tutoring for these students. Instead, we can build on our general tutoring strategies to accommodate the special traits of different students" (Soven 2006, 103). As such, the guides are making outlandish assumptions about their readers, the tutors. The assumption is that tutors will not have a learning disability or have a first language other than English, as Kiedaisch and Dinitz (2007) pointed out, but also that the tutor *and* student will likely be white, of high ability, young, and American. Telling tutors to be aware of "differences" defines "normal" sessions, too.

Moreover, when the tutoring guides include fictional scenarios of difficult sessions, the tutor is typically white, young, American, and a native English speaker. The student usually is "different." In *The St. Martin's Sourcebook*, Yaroslav, a Russian student, is hesitant to write a letter to the editor because in his country, you don't complain about the government (Murphy and Sherwood 2007, 11); Sabah is from Singapore and is hesitant to write about her teaching experiences because she doesn't want to seem boastful—it would be inappropriate in her country (12); Ted confides he has a learning disability (13); and Leonard is a non-traditional student, a manager of a trucking company for over twenty years (14). In the *Allyn and Bacon Guide*, Angela, an Asian student, writes a paper critical of Americans (Lerner and Gillespie 2003, 168–69). Though in the writing center story we tell ourselves we claim to work with all students, our positioning of us and them, as indicated in the tutoring handbooks at least, says something about our expectations about who tutors and who gets tutored, who is normal and who is different. Geller et al. come to a similar conclusion in *The Everyday Writing Center*; they write:

"As a field, we have spun a writing center narrative so universal that we don't need to think about certain matters (like identity, racism, and disenfranchisement) in the context of writing centers because our founding principles are so inherently inclusive—or so we think. Periodically, and with a regularity that signals rhythm, pace, and pattern to us, our claims to community in and through our writing centers ring hollow" (Geller et al. 2007, 13). If we paint students in this light in our official discourses—tutor training guides—it's likely that we are doing so in unofficial discourse, too.

A third consequence of the idea that a writing center is essentially a tutoring center for all students is that the story blinds us to the fact that not all students want tutoring. We can think because we exist for all students that we are the solution for all students. The numbers simply don't reflect this. The figures on the national usage of writing centers at the college level never put usage at more than 40 percent of the student populations and sometimes only about half of this. The authors of "War, Peace, and Writing Center Administration" say one-third of students use writing centers (Simpson, Braye, and Boquet 1994). "The Survey of American College Students: Use of and Satisfaction with College Tutoring Services" published in 2009 finds that just under 30 percent of students have ever used tutoring services on their campuses (Primary Research Group 2009, 20). For students majoring in education, fine arts, English, communication, and journalism, only 13–18 percent of them have ever used a tutoring service (22). Moreover, about 35 percent of students indicated it would be highly unlikely or unlikely for them to ever seek out tutoring (25).

Similar numbers can be found in the National Survey of Student Engagement (NSSE). In the 2008 report, NSSE reported on use of tutoring generally and writing centers specifically. Overall, 24 percent of highly prepared students and 38 percent of underprepared students indicate they "often" or "very often" get some sort of tutoring help (NSSE 2008, 19). In terms of writing center usage, 31 percent of first-year students indicated they took some, most, or all of their assignments to the writing center whereas just 19 percent of seniors reported the same. Writing center usage (or non-usage) was a surprising finding to the researchers of the WIDE study "The Writing Lives of College Students" as well. Of the 1,366 survey participants, 245 (18%) indicated using the writing center, and "among those participants who report working with writing center consultants, they list it as their least used collaboration. Further, participants identified collaborating with writing center consultants as least valued" (Grabill et al. 2010, 11). As a point of comparison, 86 percent of respondents to this survey used their cell phones and 67 percent used Facebook at least once for an academic *writing* task (10).

When I first found these numbers, I felt relief. The narrative of the primacy of tutoring always made me feel like I wasn't the greatest director if I wasn't each year getting more and more students through the door. I felt my ultimate goal ought to be 100 percent of students using the writing center or at least in the high 90s. We're actually around 10 percent, and I'm always quick to justify why: there's another writing center on campus in the learning center; we're out of money and space—we are operating at capacity; we do fifty-minute sessions; and students are not required to attend. I can see how my impulse to justify comes from the influence of the grand narrative. We have made each other to feel as if tutoring is most important and the only way to gauge if a writing center is successful is in how many tutoring sessions or what percentage of the population is using your center. So seeing that we are not too out of whack with national numbers—especially when our numbers are coupled with the other writing center's—I breathed a sigh of relief.

Simultaneously, when I read these numbers, I felt discouraged. I guess I've been participating in the march toward progress for so long, I now felt like we couldn't do much better than we were already doing. Not all students want tutoring. Of course, we can say among ourselves that everyone can benefit from feedback on their writing. I truly believe that. But the hard fact remains that a majority of students on our campuses will never come to our center for tutoring. Of course, there are many departments, centers, and programs on a college campus who never hope to attract more than a hundred or so students. Not every initiative ought to aim for 100 percent. However, every single student on our campuses will write. It is not as if we are an obscure minor track. Writing is central, yet most students do not want writing tutoring (and/ or they do not want tutoring the way we have conceived of it). When we say, as we do at my center, that we work with all students, we lie. We are telling a story. It's a better bet than saying that we will work with anyone but we know only about a quarter of students will take us up on our offer.

PERIPHERAL VISIONS

Not everything written about writing centers focuses exclusively on tutoring or a narrow vision of tutoring, of course. Actually, early "writing center" work described in the scholarship did not necessarily include one-to-one peer tutoring. Though locating the precise origins of today's writing center is not simple, writing center historians have revealed a diverse set of precursors in the form of labs, clinics, and auto-tutorial centers dating back to the early 1900s (see Carino 1995a; Boquet 1999; Kinkead 1996). The labs were often extensions or alternatives to classroom sites of education where teachers (or more rarely tutors) worked with small groups of students in the process of writing. Clinics, like the ones described by Robert Moore (1950), were where students could discover their own particular writing shortcomings through interviews or diagnostics with a clinician. To remedy the writing, students were given exercises to take with them. The auto-tutorials drew from both the lab and clinic, but took some of the human element out. Students worked on computers that both discovered their weaknesses and drilled them to strengthen their skills. Though quite different in approach, each of these "writing centers" all were outside of or additions to "regular" classroom instruction and each of these took improving student writing as the main goal.

Writing centers of whatever ilk were relatively rare, however, until the 1970s and 1980s, when the "new" writing center, as described by Stephen North, emerged, valuing process and offering student-centered peer-to-peer tutorials for all writers (North 1984, 69). During this time period, professionals working in writing centers were working to be seen as legitimate colleagues in their colleges and universities. To do so, Terrance Riley (as quoted in the previous chapter) notes writing center professionals "demonstrated that what they were doing was not being done by any other department or discipline; they evolved theories and discourses that highlighted their differences from other areas, and increasingly wrote only for members of their network; they amassed a body of scholarship that looked a good deal like what everyone else was producing; and on these bases they claimed a professional status often and loudly enough that they were listened to" (Riley 1994, 147). Riley suggests writing center professionals of the late twentieth century were generally successful in this endeavor.

Thus, when I visualize writing center history, I see a large, messy spiral slowly tightening and narrowing to smaller, more predictably round, neater circles. Though North's idea of the "new" writing center, among other scholarship and other professionalization efforts, gave the community a common definition to work with, it has tightened the definition of what work counts in writing centers; that is, it restricts how writing center work is storied to a very narrow range of topics. Terrance Riley describes this sort of movement as natural for emerging disciplines: "Professional success is proportional to the degree to which a discipline can overcome its mixed descent and claim a purity of purpose, while creating an environment in which its members can measure themselves according to criteria internal to the discipline" (Riley 1994, 28). Gary Olson lauded this change, saying "the writing center's chaotic adolescence is nearly over. Center directors are slowly articulating common goals, objectives, and methodologies; and writing centers are beginning to take on a common form, to evolve into a recognizable species" (Olson 1984, vii).

Yet, I find myself agreeing more with Irene Lurkis Clark, who wrote in response to Olson that she was a "bit wary of the possibility that writing centers will soon take on a 'common form' in the profession, a common form verging on dogma" (Clark 1990, 81). To be clear, I am in no way nostalgic for diagnostic centers or auto-tutorials, but it is clear to me that before the so-called "professionalization" of writing centers, before the discipline of writing center studies emerged, before these "new" writing centers, there were multiple approaches to helping writers at schools and universities, all of which were written about in the scholarship of the time that Lerner (2009) has painstakingly detailed. When writing center studies focused on a collective narrative to describe their work, they lost their sense of a mixed descent.

My visualization of a wild spiral to a narrow, precise circle describes the writing center discourse, not the complete standardization of writing center practice. Other practices for writing centers still exist. In the survey I mentioned earlier, respondents mentioned grammar labs and GED tests, and at the same time, others mentioned throwing out rigid tutoring rules and believing in magic. The spiral is still there, but the story has changed. One example of the continued variance in tutoring, despite the story that leads us to believe everyone is doing the same thing, is described in Daniel Sanford's "The Peer-Interactive Writing Center at the University of New Mexico." Here Sanford discusses his experimentation with a "peer-interactive" model, where students would come to the center to write and a tutor or two would circulate among them, offering brief moments of feedback as needed. When possible, students would be placed at tables with others working on the same assignment so they might get feedback from one another or so one tutor could address the group. This model disrupts what Sanford sees as the two defining aspects of tutorials: "First, students work one-on-one with writing consultants . . . Second, individual consultations have time constraints." (Sanford 2012, par. 3).

In addition to variance among tutoring strategies, there is evidence that centers engage in non-tutoring activities, too. Jane Nelson and Margaret Garner remark that "although an important goal of the [University of Wyoming] Writing Center is helping students with writing, its outside-of-tutoring activities are equally important and perhaps more important in regards to the faculty's vision of the Writing Center's place on campus" (Nelson and Garner 2011, 13). These outside-of-tutoring activities include class workshops and faculty workshops on teaching writing (14–15). In addition, Andrea Lunsford (2008) described open-mic nights and Saturday writing workshops for area at-risk high school students at Stanford's Writing Center in a recent keynote address. Others have noted ways to support creative writing on campus (Dvorak 2004; Adams and Adams 1994). Maria Wilson Nelson (1991) has described a short-lived small group program supporting basic and ESL writers at her writing center (also see Crosby 2006). Evidence of other non-tutoring activities—websites, videos, blogs, newsletters, podcasts, in-class introductions, workshops, and writing groups—can be found, but they are seldom theorized as something potentially pedagogically important on their own (e.g., Colpo, Fullmer, and Lucas 2000; Smith 2003; Vescio 1998; Abrams 1994; O'Hear 1983). Instead, they are mostly treated as a way to advertise or spread goodwill about the tutoring services, as a resource to use in a tutoring session, or as a resource for training tutors. The existent literature rarely posits these other activities as alternatives to tutoring or something equally important. The exception to this would be research on classroom-based tutoring that has been theorized quite extensively (see, e.g., Spigelman and Grobman 2005; Barnett and Rosen 2008) though it is often perceived as a writing across the curriculum initiative, and, of course, it is still tutoring so not entirely different from writing center tutoring itself.

Still, most of the non-tutoring work goes undocumented; non-tutoring work does not fit into the writing center grand narrative. As Bruner reminds us, "stories define the range of canonical characters, the settings in which they operate, the actions that are permissible and comprehensible. And thereby they provide, so to speak, a map of possible roles and of possible worlds in which action, thought, and self-definition are permissible (or desirable)" (Bruner 1987, 66). The current writing center grand narrative does not map non-tutoring work. In "Sites for (Invisible) Intellectual Work," Margaret J. Marshall argues that writing center work is intellectual labor even if not always recognized as such. As a first step to encourage wider acknowledgment of this point, she asserts that "the activities that go on in writing centers must be documented in order to make them visible" (Marshall 2001, 75). To document *non-tutoring* activities in writing centers, Rebecca Jackson and I undertook a survey of writing center directors in 2009 (Jackson and Grutsch McKinney 2011). We had a simple research question: What kinds of non-tutoring activities do writing centers engage in? We found that writing center directors ($n = 141$) indicated participating in almost every activity we asked about:

Almost all writing centers (81% or more) participate in these activities

- Keep records (93%)
- Provide writing handouts (89%)
- Provide workshops for students (84%)

Most writing centers (61–80%) participate in these activities

- Provide hyperlinks (79%)
- Collaborate with faculty members or departments (78%)
- Conduct satisfaction surveys (77%)
- Offer computers for student use (73%)
- Publish website (72%)
- Produce tutoring handbook (69%)
- Publish brochures (68%)
- Collaborate with writing programs (66%)
- Evaluate tutors (63%)
- Collaborate with other tutoring or support services (63%)
- Collaborate with WAC, WID, or CAC (61%)

Many writing centers (41–60%) participate in these activities

- Conduct workshops for faculty (59%)
- Collaborate with library (59%)
- Collect student demographic data (57%)
- Publish bookmarks, stickers (55%)
- Have a lending library (46%)
- Publish reports (46%)
- Publish posters (42%)

Some writing centers (21–40%) participate in these activities

- Host parties or open houses (39%)
- Serve as the subject and/or location of faculty research (39%)

- Conduct grammar/ESL drills (39%)
- Provide in-house assessment (38%)
- Collaborate with disability services (38%)
- Serve as the subject and/or location of undergraduate student research (35%)
- Create promotional items (34%)
- Create bulletin board displays (33%)
- Create lesson plans for training (30%)
- Conduct workshops for staff (29%)
- Serve as the subject and/or location of graduate student research (24%)
- Collaborate with new TA training (24%)
- Collaborate with student groups (24%)
- Offer room rental/use (23%)
- Publish newsletter (23%)
- Collect and assess retention, pass/fail, and GPA data (23%)
- Offer classes for credit (22%)

Few writing centers (0–20%) participate in these activities

- Collaborate with resident halls (19%)
- Use Facebook (18%)
- Edit/proofread (18%)
- Host conversation groups (18%)
- Sponsor writing contests (18%)
- Host lectures (17%)
- Host conferences (17%)
- Provide workshops for the community (15%)
- Provide grammar hotline (15%)
- Create training videos (15%)
- Create promotional videos (16%)
- Collaborate with teacher education (14%)
- Host writing groups (14%)
- Offer non-credit classes (13%)
- Host readings or open mics (11%)
- Provide test-taking or monitoring services (11%)
- Photocopy, etc. (10%)
- Host dissertation or thesis groups (10%)
- Publish a wiki (9%)
- Host faculty writing groups (8%)
- Blog (8%)
- Podcast (7%)
- Provide plagiarism-detection programs (7%)

- Collaborate with National Writing Project Site (6%)
- Lend laptop/equipment (6%)
- Write newspaper articles (6%)
- Share social photos (3%)
- Share social videos (3%)
- Use MySpace (2%)
- Use Twitter (2%)
- Host summer camps (2%)
- Sponsor spelling bees (1%)
- Use social bookmarking (0%)

Research like Jackson and Grutsch McKinney's (2011) and Pamela Childers's (2011) can make visible what the writing center grand narrative obscures: writing centers already do more than tutoring—a lot more. One thing that is particularly striking in the findings is that 84 percent of writing centers offer workshops for students. This suggests that the vast majority of writing centers engage in group instruction, yet our story of our work does not include this. And, importantly, since we do not see group instruction as part of our story—we do not have that visual habit—theorizing group instruction has not been in our purview. It is not one of our rhetorical habits.

The exclusive focus on tutoring has been questioned by others as well. David Coogan (1999) imagines, in *Electronic Writing Centers*, a virtual database housing student papers and offering students a way to participate in academic conversations across the country with other students writing on similar topics. Grimm (2011), Geller et al. (2007), and Weaver (2006) suggest that the writing center can be a site to combat or at least confront institutional racism. In *Noise from the Center*, Beth Boquet (2002) argues that writing centers should not be so quiet and contained; they should be more willing to challenge the status quo of the institution. And in *Facing the Center*, Harry Denny (2010) demands we pay attention to race, class, and sexuality as it plays out in our institutions. Neal Lerner (2009) argues the value of a writing laboratory approach, a precursor to contemporary writing centers, and yet a pedagogical strategy that has fallen to the wayside. Lerner reminds us there are a wide range of possibilities for teaching writing we can seek by looking to the past or looking to the future; we don't (only) have to be a tutoring center.

However, often the reaction to scholars like these who suggest that writing centers do something else or pay attention to something new is outright frustration. Writing center directors, often in tenuous positions, call uncle. "We can't do another thing!" Alternatively, directors cannot reconcile the new directions with the stories they hold about what writing centers do. Muriel Harris describes this fear when she notes, "Stretched too thin or in directions that are not appropriate to what we committed to poses an additional danger of losing our foundational principles of collaboration or active learning or interaction with students one to one" (Harris 2011, xii). I don't think, however, that widening our view on what is writing center work necessarily means doing anything new. In my opinion, we have hardly started recognizing the scope of what is already done in the writing center. So, I don't think it is fair to stick to a narrative that does not fully represent the possibility, promise, or actuality of our work on the basis that the narrative makes our work sound legible or helpful. As Bruner cautions, that which "does not get structured narratively suffers loss in memory" (Bruner 1987, 56). Should we not work to question the grand narrative, we will continue the collective forgetting of the complexity of writing center work.

6

CONCLUSION
The End of the Story or the End of the Center?

Through our talk about things, we sustain the reality of them. We are choosing what parts of the world we will orient to and we are defining what aspects of reality are most important. The question of who controls topics in our conversations is partly a question of who controls our view of the world.

—Pamela Fishman (1978), "What Do
Couples Talk about When They're Alone"

As a lover of stories, I like to ask students to write stories. In first-year composition, I often assign a family story essay. In this assignment, I ask students to tell their readers a story that is part of family lore, a story that is often repeated and that everyone in the family knows. Then I ask them to reflect on the telling of the story—who tells the story, when, and why? And, as such, what does the story or the retelling *do*? For first-year writing students, finding a story to share is usually not difficult, but the critical reflection can throw them. Students who make it to college class-rooms are typically savvy at saying what a story means—comprehending the story—but less able to say what a story does. A story just tells what happened, right?

At one point in his career, Jerome Bruner also collected family sto-ries. He became interested in autobiographies (which he calls "life sto-ries") and decided to study them by interviewing members of families since their individual stories would overlap. From this experiment, he discovered

> that the ways of telling and the ways of conceptualizing that go with [the tellings] become so habitual that they finally become recipes for structuring experience itself, for laying down routes into memory, for not only guiding the life narrative up to the present, but for directing it into the future . . . a life is not 'how it was' but how it is interpreted and reinterpreted, told and retold. (Bruner 2004, 36)

Thus, Bruner wouldn't say that "a story just happens." Stories—family stories in this case—shape our lives by how we interpret them, by how we tell them, by what they do.

Further, he argues that these stories families tell "persist stubbornly in spite of changed conditions" (Bruner 2004, 36). So even if a child changes—as children are apt to do—upon adulthood, the stories about the child remain defining characteristics of them. I have a friend, for example, who is plagued by a story her parents tell of her spendthrift ways as a teenager. Though this friend is now a couple decades beyond her teen years, gainfully employed, and careful with her money, her parents' frequent retelling of this story of her reminds her that they still think of her as a teen. "Any story one may tell about anything," Bruner writes, "is better understood by considering other possible ways in which it can be told" (Bruner 2004, 37). So, out of all the possible ways in which her parents could tell the story of my friend's financial abilities, they select out the moments that fit with the story they had been patterned to tell. We disregard, we rewrite to fit the familiar narratives.

In ways, the storyteller's discretion is like naming stellar constellations. Looking up into the vast starry heavens, one could connect the dots in an infinite number of ways. Once, though, we've been taught to find Orion's belt or the Big Dipper, it is incredibly hard not to see them. Those stars whose stories we've learned stand out to us. Those unfamiliar stars, who may be just as bright, fade because we have no story for them. In fact, sometimes I think I might see a dipper in another part of the sky simply because I've been accustomed to looking for that combination of stars.

If we think about all of this in terms of writing centers, what I've called the "writing center grand narrative" is the family (familiar) story, of writing center studies. Writing center professionals may each tell their "life stories" of their writing center work, and together we can see something of the whole in how the stories overlap. Out of all the moments that comprise our work in writing centers, writing center professionals often share those that most closely align with the grand narrative, our collective story, the rhetorical habit we have heard, that "persists stubbornly," and that shapes how we understand our work. It should not be surprising that a community of professionals has a common way of communicating; sharing a common language is actually essential for a community to exist and thrive. Problems arise when the ways in which communities communicate, their rhetorical habits, are not expansive enough to allow members to change.

In composition studies, the term/metaphor used to name how community members communicate is often *discourse community*. James Porter says a discourse community is "a group of individuals bound by a common interest who communicate through approved channels and whose discourse is regulated" (Porter 1986, 38–39). A discourse community also "shares assumptions about what objects are appropriate for examination and discussion, what operating functions are performed on those objects, what constitutes 'evidence' and 'validity,' and what formal conventions are followed" (Porter 1986, 39). Though some discourse communities can be loosely joined by conventions, many—like the writing center discourse community, I'd argue—have tightly formed rules and conventions for what is appropriate and not.[1]

David Bartholomae writes about the struggle for students to negotiate the academic discourse community—or even more specifically, the first-year writing class discourse in his now canonical essay "Inventing the University." He states: "Every time a student sits down to write for us, he has to invent the university for the occasion . . . The student has to learn to speak our language, to speak as we do, to try on the peculiar ways of knowing, selecting, evaluating, reporting, concluding, and arguing that define the discourse of our community" (Bartholomae 1985, 134). For Bartholomae, writing teachers ought to realize that when they assign essay topics, they are asking students to do something the students don't have the knowledge, yet, to participate fully in. Instead, students must "carry off the bluff" (135), by writing "a necessary and enabling fiction" in which writing teachers and students are companions and fellow researchers (136). In other words, students, or newcomers to a community more generally, do not innately know the stories of a discourse community, and lacking such knowledge, they begin with appropriation.

Both Porter and Bartholomae ask questions about how any member of a discourse community can say anything "original" when all are expected to conform to the same conventions, topics, and approaches. To point, Bartholomae, paraphrasing Barthes, states, "A writer does not write but is, himself, written by the language available to him" (Bartholomae 1985, 143). Porter says the exclusionary power of discourse communities "raises serious questions about the freedom of the writer: chiefly, does the writer have any? Is any writer doomed to plagiarism? Can any text be said to be new? Are creativity and genius actually possible?" (Porter 1986, 40). This line of questions is important.

---

1. Though Harry Denny believes "writing centers and writing center professionals might constitute a discourse community" and he is right that "we don't have collective get-togethers and negotiate terms that determine codes and membership unilaterally," most discourse communities don't. Cultural rules are rarely passed along so explicitly.

If the writing center grand narrative sets the conventions for the discourse community, how do we do tell a different story? Both Porter and Bartholomae have answers to this question, which I'll get to briefly, but first I want to note how this problem and its remedies are exasperated by the ever-beginner culture in writing center studies.

To be sure, every academic community and actually most communities have an influx of beginners who have to learn to negotiate the community mores. But writing centers are notorious for the turnover of their staffs. Undergraduates work for a year or two and then graduate. Graduate student teaching assistants may only work a semester or two before being assigned to teach a first-year writing course or given a research assistant assignment. And, importantly, administrators or professional tutors are often in contingent positions or appointed for brief (three years or less) terms (see Balester and McDonald 2001). Beginners relate to discourse communities in different ways than longer-standing members. Porter invokes Joseph Williams's term "pre-socialized cognitive states" to describe the newcomer relationship to writing for a discourse. Porter says that "pre-socialized writers are not sufficiently immersed in their discourse community to produce competent discourse: They do not know what can be presupposed, are not conscious of the distinctive intertextuality of the community, may be only superficially acquainted with explicit conventions" (Porter 1986, 42).

Likewise, Bartholomae notes, "I think that all writers, in order to write, must imagine themselves the privilege of being 'insiders'—that is, the privilege of being inside an established and powerful discourse and of being granted a special right to speak. But I think that right to speak is seldom conferred on us—on any of us, teachers or students—by virtue of that fact that we have invented or discoursed an original idea" (Bartholomae 1985, 143). He also says that a writer must "write from a position of power" in order to make an argument successfully and that requires "she must be either equal to or more powerful than those she would address" (139). Being equal to or "more powerful" or even simply being an "insider" is typically not a subject position available to beginners, and thus their contributions to the discourse, according to Bartholomae, are simply to imitate until they are able to reach insider status. Bartholomae suggests, "What our beginning students need to learn is to extend themselves, by successive approximations, into the commonplaces, set phrases, rituals and gestures, habits of mind, tricks of persuasion, obligatory conclusions and necessary connections that determine the 'what might be said' and constitute knowledge within the various branches of our academic community" (146). Yet, if a majority of those engaging in writing center discourse stay for only a few years, do they—do we—ever move beyond this? More specifically, if beginners will start by mimicking the writing center grand narrative, and so many in the community are always beginners, does this explain why the narrative has such lasting power? In Bartholomae's words, are we constantly inventing and reinventing the writing center the same way?

I do suspect that the fact that there are always more newcomers than long-standing members in the writing center community has something to do with the persistence of the story. I also think, as I have emphasized throughout, that the story makes us and others feel good. We like thinking of centers as respites away from the cold, faceless bureaucracy. It feels good to think our marginal status is by choice and not by consequence. And we feel like champions for the underclass by having tutoring as our primary mission. Further, the narrative has been the image we have presented to outsiders as well and, frankly, I don't think that writing centers have an image problem. That is to say that outsiders seem to believe that writing centers are comfortable, iconoclastic places where all students get one-to-one help on their writing. So I think that both insiders and outsiders now bolster the narrative. In truth, I think that the writing center grand narrative persists because narratives and the rhetorical and visual habits they spawn are all difficult to change. But not impossible.

In the final part of this chapter, the final chapter of the book, I want to turn toward thoughts on how a (grand) narrative can change. I'll draw on theorists who have helped me frame my argument but also on a few others whose work seems particularly insightful on change. I suppose there may be some readers who have followed along to this point, who agree that there is a grand narrative that pervades our discourse, yet who do not see a need to change it. As I mentioned in the introduction, I know getting folks to understand anything about writing centers was a battle fought for decades (and continues to be an issue in many places). For me, though, I think the writing center grand narrative has narrowed our gaze to such a degree that others do not understand the complexity of our work and we continue to face untenable positions because of it. Further, our collective research agenda is stymied both because scholars are not hired as administrators (or administrators are not paid to be scholars) and because our gaze has more or less kept us, in large part, from substantial theoretical and empirical research on aspects of writing center work beyond tutoring.

Here's where I can insert a whopper of a cliché: acknowledging the problem is the first step. As much as I'd like to say something more profound than this, I'm afraid this about sums it up. Acknowledging that the writing center grand narrative is a representation—not *how it is*, as Bruner (2004) reminds us—is really the first step. That step allows for the possibility that not all is represented; some things are left out. Hayden White reveals the paradox that narratives seem complete even as they leave things out: "Every narrative, however seemingly full, is constructed on the basis of a set of events that might have been included but were left out; this is as true of imaginary narratives as it is of realistic ones. And this consideration permits us to ask what kind of notion of reality authorizes construction of a narrative account of reality in which continuity rather than discontinuity governs the articulation of the discourse" (White 1987, 10).

Thankfully, there is more that can be done than just this acknowledgment. For one, both Bruner and Lyotard have some faith in individual stories. Lyotard says in an interview with Gary Olson, "If we are vigilant against master narratives, it means precisely that we try to consider the small narratives of specific groups" (Olson and Lyotard 1995). This impulse is perhaps familiar from collections such as *Stories from the Center* and *CompTalk*. The idea behind these is to let the people tell their stories. Likewise, Bruner notes that "narratives do accrue and, as anthropologists insist, the accruals eventually create something variously called a 'culture' or a 'history' or, more loosely, a 'tradition'" (Bruner 1991b, 56). So if we make a point of collecting or hearing individual stories, we might add instantiations of counterstories to the grand narrative. Or we'll get more instantiations of it since it is hard to write for a discourse community while defying the conventions of it.

But Porter is more hopeful. He writes that "every new text has the potential to alter the Text in some way; in fact, every text admitted into a discourse community changes the constitution of the community— and discourse communities can revise their discursive practices" (Porter 1986, 41). So after acknowledging that stories are representations, the second possibility for change seems to be almost as simple: write. If the grand narrative does not tell my story, I need to tell it. Sure, I may be the only one interested in, say, using social media to change faculty perceptions of writing center work, but if I write about it, others might begin to care also. Others might write back. Soon, there's a contingency of members in the community who see the value of that sort of writing center work.

A particular type of writing can be effective at dislodging grand narratives. In *Community Action and Organizational Change*, Brenton Faber showcases his attempts to bring forth change in various organizations. In each situation, he helps the members of the organization see how the discourse and narratives surrounding the organization work against the goals and values of the organization. Faber suggests writing can change things "when people transgress genres, violate boundaries, and intentionally break with routine practices, change becomes a possibility" (Faber 2002, 172). Faber, thus, encourages writing that is different from convention in genre, topic, and substance in order to change discourse conventions (what insiders use) and to change perception of outsiders—the discourse surrounding a community or organization.

Likewise, toward the end of Fleckenstein's *Vision, Rhetoric, and Social Action in the Composition Classroom*, she asks a question that is similar to what I'm asking here. She wonders, "How does a member of a culture, immersed in the visual and discursive regimes of that culture, imagine a different reality and a different selfhood in ways that do not replicate the old matrices of abuse and the subjectivity of victim (or victimizer)?" (Fleckenstein 2010, 114). The answer she settles on is that people need agency that is equal parts imagination and faith. People must "be able to imagine and believe themselves as agents before acting as agents" (114). Fleckenstein offers several rhetorical and visual strategies for disrupting "old matrices" including contradiction. She writes: "Contradiction erupts within the visual narrative because any narrative—verbal or visual—is sewn together out of bits and pieces of images . . . We sift through a bewildering kaleidoscope of images, picking and choosing what to attend to and how to respond to those selected images . . . However, all those bits and pieces we leave out press for attention. They put pressure on the tenuous narrative unity so that disorder and incoherence erupt" (125). Despite the violent imagery, Fleckenstein sees the eruption of narrative unity as a good thing. In a similar vein, Geller et al. (2007) suggest the trickster administrator or tutor can do the same for rote writing center practices: the trickster can disrupt.

Once when I was in graduate school, I enrolled in a community education drawing class at the local community college. I had completed my coursework and wanted to do something that balanced all of the time I spent in my head working on my dissertation. The teacher had us use a book called *Drawing on the Right Side of the Brain* by Betty Edwards (1999). The book's premise is that when many of us sit down to draw, we draw based on ideas in our minds instead of drawing what is in front of us.

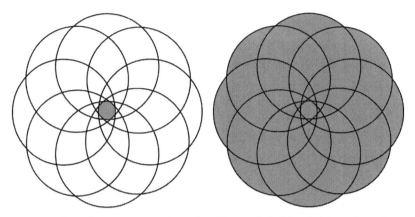

Figure 6.1. Tunnel vision: narrow vision of writing center work

Figure 6.2. Peripheral vision: widened purview of writing center work

We have accepted communal drawing habits, if you will, that guide us toward drawing representations of objects yet keep us from drawing the objects as they appear to us. One manifestation of this is how our brain interferes with our vision. We can look at a profile of someone and only see one side of his or her face. Our brain may intrude with the information that the person has two eyes and before you know it we're adding to our drawing the eye we don't actually see but know to be there. It sounds bizarre and I for one didn't really think our minds—particular our socially wired minds—could interfere with our vision. Time and time again, however, the drawing instructor walked from student to student asking us to erase what we'd added to our still life that we'd added in with our minds. The best technique to counter the contrary messages we receive from our eyes and from our minds is to not actually think about drawing the object but to instead focus on drawing the space around the object—drawing the negative space. This means not trying to intentionally draw an object dimensional, but to draw the shape of the object as if it were on a two-dimensional plane. The book warns that this way of seeing can be so disruptive of our typical ways of seeing that our heads can hurt and we can feel nauseous.

Thus, drawing the negative space requires changing visual habits. The change is disruptive enough to our equilibrium that our bodies may react. I've argued throughout this book that our rhetorical habits—particularly our story of writing center work—has conditioned us to narrow visual habits, and encourages a tunnel vision. So perhaps Betty Edwards provides us with a concrete directive in changing vision. Instead of telling the story of writing centers based on what we imagine is there based on our communal habits of storying writing centers, maybe we should study closely what we do see and trace the negative space around that so we get a sense of what writing centers are not.

At conferences, I often hear writing center professionals use the first-person plural when invoking a writing center trope for which the speaker believes there will be consensus. These moments are often marked with an opening like "In writing centers, we . . ." or "As writing center people, we . . ." My ears always perk up at these moments because they reveal something about what speakers believe will be universally held truths about writing centers and writing center work. I think too long we've been focused on what we have in common; this reinforces a tunnel vision by suggesting there's only value in discussing what is universal. The writing center grand narrative encourages this stance. Yet, if we were to visualize this, we might see more clearly what gets left out. Imagine, for instance, that each writing center in the world were a circle in a complex Venn diagram. Each circle contained all of the work of the center. The various writing centers (circles) would certainly overlap—writing centers do share common practices. When all of the circles were mapped, there would remain a small space in which all circles overlapped, indicating the practices or tenets (believed to be) universally held. (See Figure 6.1 for a simplified version of this.) That small gray area is frequently imagined as the purview of writing center studies. Instead, a Betty Edwards approach would ask that we trace the outside of the entire diagram, the negative space, to see the actual dimensions of writing center work and operational beliefs. (See Figure 6.2.) In that vision, anything that any center is doing is considered "writing center work." We do not limit ourselves to writing about what we share in common. When I think of a tunnel vision or a peripheral vision for writing centers, this is what I picture.

A theme running through this entire book is the idea of belonging. I have come to see a paradox in how we articulate our belonging in the writing center community. We draw on the writing center grand narrative to reveal our belonging. The narrative is our rhetorical habit, and it shapes our visual habits. But the more that I participate in the writing center grand narrative, the more I feel alone. The writing center grand narrative does not represent the whole of my lived experience as a writing center professional—nor yours, I'm guessing. Taking the effort to acknowledge how the narrative operates, writing transgressions of the narrative, allowing the suppressed and peripheral pieces to surface, and re-envisioning the boundaries of writing center work will allow us to dislodge our established rhetorical and visual ways.

If we don't dislodge the writing center grand narrative, what we now conceive of as writing center studies is going to fracture. Picture those Venn diagrams cracking into pieces and falling off the page. Practices and theories not (believed to be) embraced by all—not in that small inner square—will find another organizing structure to append to. As Fleckenstein reminds us, the "bits and pieces we leave out press for attention" (Fleckenstein 2010, 125.) In the last decade, two distinct developments have already begun to "press" for attention. The first is the multiliteracy centers movement. Multiliteracy centers have various configurations and names but they are typically based on a writing center model of peer feedback, providing students with feedback on a variety of texts on a variety of platforms—not just essays in MS Word files (see Sheridan and Inman 2010). Some multiliteracy centers also stress the importance of tutoring in writing, understanding the cultural implications of any literacy project, and embrace multiple Englishes (Balester et al. 2012). Some scholars, like Murphy and Hawkes, suggest that "the future of the Writing Center is not as a Writing Center but as a multiliteracy center with expanded pedagogical possibilities and new roles for Writing Center specialists" (Murphy and Hawkes 2010, 175). While others argue that writing centers should remain writing centers, expanding their practices instead of spawning new centers (Grutsch McKinney 2009, 2010; Balester et al. 2012). Regardless, the multiliteracy movement is pushing.

The second movement that is pressing on the disciplinary boundaries is the transition of writing centers into centers for writing excellence (CWEs) or "comprehensive writing centers" (Isaacs 2011, 131). CWEs, generally, articulate a broader mission than a writing center might. Typically, in addition to peer tutoring for students, CWEs might have faculty workshops and retreats, campus events focused on writing, and instruction for improving the teaching of writing on campus. Robert Koch says this movement is the third "seismic shift" to come to writing centers after the enrollment shift and the technology shift (Koch 2011, 152–53). When Isaacs writes that "a trope that writing center administrators need to break out of is the idea that they must be accommodating and, most importantly, modest" (Isaacs 2011, 137), she is showing just how much in her estimation the CWE presses on the writing center narrative as she believes CWEs "are the opposite of modest" (131). The writing center story, for Isaacs, is too narrow to contain a CWE.

In both of these instances, should the idea of a writing center—the story of writing centers—be inflexible to expansion, what we conceive of as writing center studies will split. Multiliteracy centers will go in one direction and CWEs the other. Left will be the narrow tunnel vision of writing center work. It is just as plausible that one of these notions will dominate and slowly subsume the writing center community, a replay of the 1970s and 1980s when writing *centers* subsumed writing *labs* and writing *clinics*.

Since the writing center grand narrative is problematic—it has obfuscated material realities, it has perpetuated subpar conditions for writing centers and writing center professionals, and it has restricted the subject of writing center theory and research too narrowly—it is with more than wistful nostalgia that makes me root for a new story over a new center. To riff on Gardner and Ramsey (2005), the writing center grand narrative has outlived its usefulness. Now is the time for peripheral visions.

APPENDIX: SURVEY RESULTS

This section contains the results of an online survey I conducted in April 2011. (Analysis of this survey can be found in Chapter 4.) One hundred seventeen respondents participated in the survey. Responses have not been modified or corrected except to remove identifying information.[1]

Question 1. What is your current status/position? Select all that apply.

Tutor	42	36%
Writing center administrator (director, coordinator, assistant director, etc.)	54	46%
Faculty	24	21%
Professional staff	5	4%
Graduate student	13	11%
Undergraduate student	22	19%
Other	7	6%

[Participants may select more than one checkbox, so percentages may add up to more than 100%.]

Question 2. What type of school do you work at?

Elementary school	0	0%
Secondary school	11	9%
Community college (2yr)	16	14%
Public college/university (4yr+)	50	43%
Private college/university (4yr+)	37	32%
Other	3	3%

---

1.   One question and responses were omitted from this section and from the analysis.

Question 3. Does your center communicate a description of your writing center to those at your school in any of the following ways?

Brochures, bookmarks, posters, bulletin boards, other print materials	109	93%
Institutional website	107	91%
Facebook, blog, or other non-institutional web presence	49	42%
Videos	39	33%
Class tours and/or intro-ductions	95	81%
Emails to faculty, staff, or students	101	86%
Reports	61	52%
Workshops for faculty, staff, or students	84	72%
Meetings or informal con-versations	91	78%
None of these	1	1%
Other	20	17%

[Participants may select more than one checkbox, so percentages may add up to more than 100%.]

Question 4. In your own words, what is a writing center?

A writing center is a space—intellectual, physical, emotional—where writers come together to discuss writing, with one writer playing the role of giving feedback to other writers (individuals or groups).

A writing center is a place where students can work with tutors to focus on becoming a better writer. They are places for thinking, arguing, discussing, and growing.

A place where ready audiences await developing texts.

A writing center provides assistance and support to writers in a safe, confidential environment. That assistance can take place at any (or all) stages of the writing process.

It's a friendly space where students can go to have a conversation about writing.

A writing center is a place for student-writers to find assistance, encouragement, and support for their writing.

A writing center is a welcoming, collaborative place—brick and mortar, online, or both—where writers of all skill levels, interests, and disciplines can gather, exchange and receive feedback during the writing process, and receive support and encouragement from tutors, staff, and fellow student writers. I also think the 21st Century writing center focuses on the community and culture of writing and acknowledges that there are numerous ways to communicate meaning and interpretation of a text (be it written, visual, or multimodal).

A writing center is a place that offers students space to talk through their ideas and their issues with writing. At the writing center, students learn the benefits of having a "sounding board" for their thoughts and also learn skills that help them be better editors and proofreaders of their own writing.

The mission of a writing center is to help students create acceptable texts for academic writing. In so doing, our objectives are to help students become more confident about their writing and provide them with a "tool box" to approach any kind of writing situation that they may encounter, both in classes and the world of work.

It's a place for students to get feedback on their writing from other students. It's a place where the students and the tutors learn collaboratively.

A writing center is both a physical space as well a service offered to writers, usually within the confines of a high school or college campus. As a space, it should be accessible to everyone, will hopefully reflect the latest technology that students need to write effectively, and should contain many resources to help writers write, such as handbooks, house-designed handouts, and the all-important coffee pot. As a service, writing centers should provide an audience for writers who can respond thoughtfully to their work. This "audience" can consist of peers, graduate students, and other professional tutors, but the power dynamics in a session should be considered as thoughtfully as possible to create a comfortable environment where writers can open up and share their concerns about their work.

A place inviting students to engage in collaborative learning to improve their academic skills, as well as general critical thinking and critical reading skills.

A place where the focus is on process rather than result.

A writing center provides one-on-one consultancy services for writers at all stages of the writing process.

A space or encounter where two or more writers come together over texts. At its best, these writers come as peers, that is with the understanding that each brings expertise, though usually different expertise. Also, at its best, neither has a "grading" role.

A writing center is a place where students can come at any stage of their writing to have someone with training in writing respond to their writing needs.

A writing center is a safe space where students can receive help with writing as well as learn about taking ownership of their academic work. A writing center is also a body of resources related to all stages of the writing process. Moreover, writing centers are places where individuals can practice and hone tutoring skills that will be beneficial in an array of career paths. Basically, it is the premiere space for sharing and collaborating in an academic institution.

A place where writers can get help/feedback with their writing, any where in the process.

Integral part of the writing program, where students from all disciplines can receive helpful feedback on writing-assignments.

A place where students can come to meet with an interested reader to talk about their writing and improve their writing.

A writing center is a collaborative space where writers can work on their writing at any stage of the writing process, brainstorming, drafting, revising, editing. Using tutoring strategies that focus on developing better writers (long-term goal) rather than better papers (short-term goal) is a key part of the writing center mission.

A center for anything writing related on a campus—any kind of writing, any stage in the writing process, any level of writer. Writing support, tutoring, workshops, events, etc. can all fit under this.

A space and time where collaborative work in reading/responding to writing occurs.

A space that connects writers with readers.

A place where students can get a second pair of eyes to look over their paper, to focus on higher order issues or to work on specific grammar problems. To help make better writers.

A place where writers work together to help each other.

A writing center is a place where any writing can come to talk about their writing at any stage in their writing process. Ideally it is a place that focuses on learning and improving as a writer.

The writing center is a place and a pedagogy. As a place it provides comfort, support, and growth to writers. As a pedagogy, the writing center steps between the writer and the instructor to give the writer knowledgeable guidance that promotes confidence and increasing skill without judgment.

A writing center is a haven where students can feel comfortable sharing and discussing their writing. It is a place of comfortable learning, where students and tutors alike often gain more from their time together than either expected.

It is a center to obtain help with writing of any type.

The writing center is a place of collaborative learning for writing and other forms of communication, including, but not limited to, group projects/presentations, poster creation, deep reading and researching skills, and spoken communication(s). We strive to make people more confident communicators, not to make A papers.

A community of writers working together to practice and improve writing skills.

A writing center is simultaneously a place, a pedagogy, and a community of practice of writers. A writing center promotes certain habits of mind or dispositions—such as active listening, life-long learning, collaborative decision-making, self-reflection, among other beliefs that suggest an understanding that knowledge is provisional and open to negotiation.

A place where people can go to write or seek help or feedback on their writing.

A writing center is a learner-centered environment where writers can go to have conversations with tutors in order to learn about, develop and grow their writing process.

A writing center is a nexus for academic literacy. It is a place where writers gather to collaborate, co-teach, and consult with each other. While the world at large trumpets the importance and centrality of writing as a skill, ability, and necessity, writing centers are the place where that noise becomes real work.

A writing center is a place where students can get help with any part of the communication process, whether it be brainstorming, revising, or visual and oral presentations. Students may also come in order to better understand reading materials, where tutors may help with close reads and annotating text. The writing center is open to a diverse group of students and alumni, such as native and non-native English speakers, and students across all majors.

A place where students receive instruction/assistance with writing projects/assignments. A resource for faculty to aid students in the writing process.

A place on campus that promotes the values associated with good writing of all kinds (including multimedia writing, for example, or non-academic writing) and that provides individualized instruction in writing.

To me, a writing center is a collaborative environment to help students of all ages and fields with their writing, regardless of topic or class.

A writing center is a space at which students receive tutoring from faculty, staff, and/or their peers on issues specific to writing.

A place where students can come and get help/direction on their own writing and individual writing needs.

A writing center is a place on campus where more experienced and skilled writers help other students improve their writing, brainstorm ideas, revise, and workshop. It is not a remedial place, it is not a classroom.

A place where students can come and receive peer tutoring and where the goal is to create a better writer, not just better papers.

A writing center is a space where writers come to talk out and collaboratively experiment with ideas.

A writing center is a place where people of a university, no matter their writing background, can receive assistance on writing. This is a place to become better writers, not just to make a writing better.

A Writing Center is a safe space where writers can come to gain inspiration for brainstorming, outlining, revising, or polishing literary projects. This can range from a productive conversation about the topic, or an extra read-through by a fresh set of eyes.

Where students come to sharpen their writing skills for both academic and personal growth.

A Burkean parlor where student writers converse and collaborate on any and all subjects. Sometimes there is a text; sometimes there is no.

A writing center is a place where writers (tutors and students) explore together the charm and the difficulty of writing. A writing center should nurture people to become individual, independent writers, who learn how to think, how to articulate themselves, and how to ask for and offer help.

A student-directed space where writers can talk about their writing and help each other.

A place on campus that provides writing support.

A place where any member of the community can come to get help with writing-at any time during the process: planning, drafting, revising, editing, etc.

A safe place for writers to support other writers in the art and craft of expression.

A writing center is a service for faculty and students. It allows students and faculty to talk through their ideas to develop a better understanding of what they want to do with a writing assignment. That could mean for faculty how they develop and assess assignments. For students it may mean anything from talking through their thoughts to providing clarification on mechanical issues in a piece of writing. It's a way for people to grow as writers and thinkers. For the school it is a way to develop cohesiveness among the faculty & consistency throughout the curriculum.

A writing center (either a physical or virtual location) provides support to help students become better writers. Writing centers are staffed by tutors who are often, but not exclusively, peer tutors. Tutors work collaboratively with students on any writing task, in any stage of the writing process. Although tutors and students will discuss writing within the context of a project, tutors and students should move beyond the end result of a single project to how those skills are transferrable to other writing contexts.

A writing center is a place where tutors can aid students in writing.

A writing center is a place where people come to get one-on-one help to improve their writing skills.

A writing center is a supplemental resource to reinforce what students learn in class and which provides students with information, materials, and tutors to help with any stage of the writing process for any course.

Both a physical or virtual locus for the support of student/staff/faculty writing/communicating endeavors and an approach to teaching and learning (student-centered, hands-on, collaborative) that can be exported to other physical or virtual environments.

A place for students to have conversations about their writing in order to improve as writers.

A place for discussion, collaboration, and guidance in writing of all kinds.

To me, a writing center is a "center" for writing on campus. It's a place where writers (students, staff, faculty) can come at any stage of the their writing process to get feedback, advice, and/or simply the perspective of another reader. It's also a place where tutors can develop as writers and as practitioners. Even as I write the above words, they seem to simplify what my writing center (any writing center) is. I think a writing center is not simply a place or a group of people but it is a complex ecology influenced by a myriad of factors—the institution, the center's place within the institution, the people who work their, their literacy experiences, the writers who come in the door, etc. etc. (You get the idea.)

A place where writers talk about writing. The good, the bad and the ugly.

A writing center is a formally organized entity—usually affiliated with and contained within a larger educational institution(s)—at which individuals may receive a variety of types of coaching to improve their abilities to communicate via the written word.

A positive and supportive place where people can work to expand their communication skills with peers.

A writing center is a collaborative, supportive space for writers of all levels to interact and support one another with the writing process at all stages.

A place where students can go to brainstorm for, and receive feedback on, academic and creative writing assignments.

Primarily a resource to provide assistance to students who have questions or problems relating to writing (and reading), most often associated with classwork. It is not a writing mechanics correction service or focused on particular assignments/subject matter. The scope for our center also includes work with members of the community who sometimes bring resumes, cover letters, and various applications.

A place for all writers to talk about their writing, at any stage of the writing process. A place where writers come to discover and develop ideas, figure out how to make good rhetorical choices, and develop metacognitive awareness about the writing process.

A place where people go to talk through their writing needs, from thinking through publishing, with other writers who just happen to be good at and trained to draw out improvement through questioning and understanding.

A place where students, faculty, and staff can go to talk about their writing and writing concerns with tutors.

A place where the aim of one-to-one tutoring is for learning to occur, in the context of the act of writing. In a writing center, each learner and each writing task are regarded as unique; no assumptions are made about what writers should already know. In a writing center, learning is separated from evaluation for grades and from pre-determined schedules. In a writing center, learning is a two-way event, so that both writer and tutor should be learning.

A place where students come for help and support with their writing. A comfort zone for improvement in learning. A source of information (consultations, workshops) for faculty and students in all disciplines. A place for research into writing, learning, and teaching practices.

At the university level, writing centers are voluntary, one-on-one support (ideally) provided by composition instructors over the course of an entire post-secondary career. Peer tutors are not necessary, but add a different form of psychological comfort (for some). One an individual level, writing centers are a collection of professional and trained staff willing and able to provide constructive feedback on writing tasks or, preferably, an intellectually vigorous conversation about the content and form of a student's writing. But what a writing center "is" comes from my experience. What a writing center "should be" is often, in ways subtle and overt, much different. My ideal writing center helps make students intellectual and civic samurai, able to confidently manage and execute any and all forms of communication. Of course, this mentality combines both the process and rhetorical approaches to writing . . . (which I already see leads me to the next question).

A safe haven for students to go over their work with a teacher different from their classroom teachers. It is a place to get fresh ideas, some repair work, and morale boost to reassure students that they can rethink all those red marks.

A space where writers and readers come together to talk about, work on, and support writing.

A location where individuals with background in writing (whether that background comes from a tutor training course or staff meetings or on-the-job training) engage in conversation primarily one-to-one to help writers learn to improve their writing choices and rhetorical understanding/insights.

A writing center is a place where students can go to improve their writing skills.

A writing center is a place open to the surrounding community (e.g., campus community, student body) to which people can come for advice, discussion, and learning concerning papers and writing.

Every writer needs a reader . . . and a listener and a talker. Our Writing Center serves the greater college and community by being an open, friendly and approachable place where writers can have conversations about their papers. We offer assistance, advice, guidance and suggestions on everything from content and organization, to grammar, punctuation, and citing. But most of all, we listen and engage writers in conversations about their own writing. Through these conversations, together, we often stumble upon new pieces of information that the writer adds to the essay, enhancing it's readability and "value" to the writer. In the end, we strive to have every writer more engaged with their writing when they leave our Writing Center than when they entered it.

And, if they learned something along the way, all the better. In any case, we know that if they leave thinking about their own writing, understanding that writing is a process that we learn and grown from, then they will be back and we can continue our conversations with them another day.

My definition as a WC Director in two schools was "The Writing Center is a low-risk environment where there is a reverence for writing."

A writing center is an institution designed to assist and support students outside of the classroom. It provides an intimate setting for those who attend a college or university in America to seek peer advice on developing a stronger voice in the art of English composition.

A writing center is a place (either actual or virtual) that supports students in their development in written communication. This could occur through individual instruction or group instruction, provision of material or human resources, elf-paced or guided/directed instruction. It could be aimed at filling in the gaps in a student's understanding and skills, or by stretching the boundaries of an already skilled writer. Student development in written communication could be achieved by working with students directly or by indirectly helping them by supporting faculty development. is defined by its aims and not by how it achieves those aims.

A friendly community of writers sharing ideas, skills, problems, solutions, and encouraging support.

A Writing Center is a place in a college or university where students come to discuss their writing. The writing tutors can be fellow students, but not always. The Writing Center is a wonderful place where ANYTHING can be talked about, whether it's the content of the paper, the mechanics of writing, the assignment, and even the instructor! :-)

A writing center is a place that facilitates and encourages both faculty and students to be better writers by providing the support and resources necessary to do that.

Writing centers provide a safe, open space for writers of all levels to receive support for their writing projects—anything from a personal statement or resume, thesis or dissertation, and the odd hometown newspaper column written for their favorite charity.

Provides one-on-one assistance to support students as they become better writers.

A writing center is a place where students (broadly defined) come for feedback about writing projects. Sometimes students bring already drafted material but other times they come to brainstorm, to talk, to think, or even to vent frustrations. A writing center is a place where two (or more) people talk about writing and writing projects and attempt to move that writing project forward.

A center for writing (duh!): that means, we work on any kind of writing, and with any constituent who has a writing task or project.

A place where students can get one-on-one assistance with writing projects of any kind, and a place where students interested in writing can find resources to further and develop their interests.

A physical space in which writers (tutors and students) discuss writing and writing processes.

A writing center is a place where students can get together to talk about writing, a discussion that certainly is intended to move forward the student writer seeking help, but will also allow the student tutor to better understand how to talk about writing.

A writing center is a community-driven education establishment based on collaboration between community members (peers and/or writing specialists) to further the goal of improved literacy in the community the center serves.

A comfortable environment in which writers can work with trained "coaches" to improve their writing skills.

A space and the people that provide support for students, administrators, and faculty to the purpose of the improvement of writing and writing pedagogy in an academic environment but also with wider implications.

A place of ideas more than a place of purely writing essentials. Our job at this writing center is to help synthesize ideas and let the clients do the thinking on their own rather than give them a page number in a handbook or correcting comma faults.

A writing center is among the most important places on campus. It is a student-centered area where those who write for school-related and personally-related purposes can receive guidance and reviews of their work, as well as someone on which to "bounce off" ideas for writing. The writing center should be equipped to handle typical student-related needs for advice and information.

A place where students can go to get help on papers or gain general knowledge to improve their writing skills.

A place for students of all levels to come for help with writing in all disciplines and at all stages of writing.

A writing center is a place that fosters writer agency through conversations on composing.

A W C is a resource, for all the University's students and faculty, to help improve the understanding and practice of the various writing processes and products that a University requires. As such, it should also ideally conduct its own research and serve as the University's expert voice on writing in and across the disciplines.

A writing center is a space (geographic or cyber) where clients and consultants collaborate to improve writing skills for all levels of writers across disciplines.

A writing center is a place where students learn to become better writers.

A writing center is a place where students can go to talk about writing in all its facets—understanding and valuing the assignment, sorting and evaluating sources, pre-writing, outlining, organizing, revising, questioning, editing, citing, and the list goes on.

A place where students of any level of academic ability can come to meet with peer tutors in order to improve their writing.

The writing center is where those educated in writing center theory and practice help writers learn to use language more effectively, produce clear writing appropriate to their purposes and audiences, and develop positive attitudes about writing and about themselves as writers. A writing center is where students become consultants who are curious about writers and their writing, committed to the generative possibilities of diversity in ideas and people, proactive about their own learning and professional development, and cultivating a "show me some evidence" attitude about the world.

A writing center is where student writers can talk with their peers in order to work through their writing process and their papers. It is not a place to solely fix grammar, but to discuss ideas and rhetorical strategies to make for better writing. A writing center also gives the student authority over the paper rather than rewriting the paper for the student.

A place where people can go to get help with their writing.

A writing center is a place where one can come and get help for their writing, or come to get knowledge about the resources which are available to them about what writing can do for them.

A writing center is a place where students seek guidance, bringing their words and ideas, in order to become better writers.

It is a place where students can bring their writing, and where they can get suggestions on how to improve a piece or help brainstorming how to start one.

Question 5. How do you describe the role of your writing center to those at your own school?

We work to support student success in relation to writing.

Our writing center has been shifting in the last year or two from being more of a "mentor giving feedback" to a "co-writer giving feedback" and from consultants relying almost solely on intellectual tools to consultants relying equally on emotional, personal, affective tools, including the physical space and of course our ever-present peanut M&Ms. :)

We help students become better writers through 30-minute sessions. We encourage students to make repeat visits to continue improving their skills as well as their product.

The Writing Center exists to show novice writers how to cross the divide between naive writing and more expert writing. It exists to provide all writers a ready audience.

It is a place to come for help with sentence level problems in a draft, It is a place to come with complicated problems in writing or composing a piece of writing. Sometimes it is a place to come for confidential advice about a writing class or a writing teacher.

Our writing center's role is to help students at all levels with their writing concerns.

I tell students and professors that the writing center helps students of all ability levels with writing in all subjects and disciplines and all aspects of the writing process.

We tell our online learning community that the writing center is a safe and nurturing place where students can discover self-directed learning objects, participate in synchronous and asynchronous tutoring, and discuss their writing with caring and qualified professional tutors.

The writing center offers coaching services to students to give them the tools they need to become better academic writers. We don't offer a proofreading service, since our goal is to enable students to become better editors and proofreaders of their own writing.

About two minutes ago, I had a conversation with a student who uses the writing center, and her words were that she never would have made it to graduation next month without our help; we are a lifesaver to students who need and want our support; we are a way to find help for students to professors; although we are student-centered, we provide help to professors with their own writing.

A lot of faculty think it's a place to send students for proofreading. A lot of students probably think it's for weak writers. The students who go regularly and the writing faculty see it as a place for every writer to get feedback and improve.

Our writing center is first and foremost a place where ALL writers can get excellent feedback about their work, regardless of where they are in the writing process or how confident they feel in their own writing. We encourage all of our tutees to grow comfortable with the act of writing and never look down on them for needing help, if that's what happens in a session. Over the years we've tried to cultivate that we are not a remedial service and that all writers need an audience to improve their work.

My role is to build as many connections and collaboration partners around campus as possible, in order to facilitate easy access for students, and to put a focus on different ways to teach writing and think about it.

We provide a free service to students who primarily come on their own initiative to have their drafts read and commented upon.

A space or encounter where two or more writers come together over texts. At its best, these writers come as peers, that is with the understanding that each brings expertise, though usually different expertise. Also, at its best, neither has a "grading" role.*

The responses marked with * indicate where a respondent put the same response for this question as they did for the previous question ("what is a writing center?").

Our writing center is a place where students can come to have a very knowledgeable and experienced tutor respond to their writing with probing questions that help a student become a better writer.

We describe our center as a place that does so much more than proof-read. Our center is not called a writing center, so many times we simply explain that we are the writing center for our college.

A place where writers can get help/feedback with their writing, any where in the process.

To help students from all disciplines communicate better through writing and to help them become better writers.

You can come get help on your writing at any stage of the writing process—brainstorming, outlining, drafting, rough draft, almost final draft. It's great for dissertators because you can set up weekly appointments for mini-deadlines.

Our writing center supports students from various disciplines across campus (probably mostly in disciplines beyond English). Originally, we were started to support Writing Intensive courses, but we are only minimally succeeding in seeing those students.

Primarily to tutor students in the their writing through individual or small group tutorials and workshops. Secondarily to conduct faculty and staff oriented trainings and events to improve writing awareness and writing-related practices around the campus.

A space and time for collaborative peer learning as a way to enhance writing instruction across the disciplines and curriculum.

A non-evaluative space for undergraduate students to receive feedback on their writing. [Name]

I'd like to make a broader claim that would reflect my beliefs about writers/readers, but right now I'm restricted from serving anyone but undergraduate students.

A place where students can get a second pair of eyes to look over their paper, to focus on higher order issues or to work on specific grammar problems. To help make better writers.*

Teaching, helping, learning, sharing.

The writing center helps students to succeed as students and improve as writers.

Our role is support and knowledgeable guidance without evaluation.

The writing center is vital, especially for our first year students and international student community. Its is somewhere they can come to learn without having to worry about being constantly judged.

One of the most benefical programs at our university. Without it, I would have never gotten through my first year. I am now in my third year and use them often.

The writing center is a place of collaborative learning for writing and other forms of communication, including, but not limited to, group projects/presentations, poster creation, deep reading and researching skills, and spoken communication(s).

Our writing center is one of many tutoring centers on campus. We see a lot of international students and expository students. Our faculty support is mixed: English teaching assistants seem to recommend us highly to their students, while professors within the English department have varied responses and those outside of the department are largely unaware of the work we do.

We offer feedback to writers at all stages in the writing process and on all kinds of writing. We are also a laboratory for student research on our campus because research is a crucial part of our peer tutoring program.

I think most people view it as a place to get help if you're enrolled in the expos program.

The Writing Center is a collaborative learning environment where trained tutors engage writers in conversations about their writing. In order to make the most out of a tutoring appointment, writers are encouraged to come in with specific questions about their writing.

The writing center offers one-to-one writing consultation with all University students—graduate, undergraduate, and professional.

Writers can bring any writing project—whether academic, professional, or personal—at any stage. The writer sets the agenda and the consultant will address the specific ideas, questions, and concerns the writer brings up.

I tell students that they can come to the Writing Center for any stage of the writing process that they are in, and that they don't need to always have a piece of writing in their hands. I also emphasize that we can help them with close reads and understanding written material. The most important thing that I tell students is that the writing center helps students become stronger, more confident writers, and the role of the tutor is not to simply "fix" their work. Instead, I focus on a more collaborative process to improving the student's work.

It is a useful tool for those who need writing assistance.

Support for all kinds of writing and speaking for faculty as well as students, a place to promote and support and research rhetoric and writing and their pedagogy.

I would say that I'm a tutor in writing, that I'm able to talk to a student, peer to peer, regarding their paper and help them with it in any way I can. I don't believe by any means that it makes me a person of authority, but rather just a person with a very colorful writing background.

I tutor other students with the goal of helping them become better writers in the process of improving the work they bring to the session.

A place where students can collaborate and work together to improve one's writing ability.

Our writing center is very involved in the first year writing program. We have tutors to help anyone on campus with any type of writing, but we mostly end up working with students who are required to come for a class or have been recommended to see us by a teacher.

As a place where anyone can go get help with writing. I describe it as really helpful, not just an editing service, etc. I tell people that the tutors are very nice and there's always coffee!

Our writing center is frightfully small for the large population of students that we are supposed to be serving; however, those who do use the service often return repeatedly. Students seem to find the time, attention, and relaxed space valuable for improving written communication.

Used to support all students of different disciplines, but also gives special support to First Year Writing students taking basic courses.

I think my writing center is sometimes misunderstood. I think those who have the best idea of what we do are specific "enlightened" or well-informed professors and first-year students who come in without preconceived notions or the baggage of grade pressure. I think sometimes the writing center ends up being an excuse for professors or students to not work with one another on an assignment in an important way, more of as a "fix-it" shop than the powerful tool it can be. But I think overall that our writing center does a great job of acting as a sort of safe haven or rescue boat to throw out a preserver to struggling students. All of us tutors have felt overwhelmed with a writing project before, and I think our center serves as an honest place to address and conquer those fears in a manageable and realistic way.

As a very helpful resource, no matter your education level.

Quite frankly I gave up long ago. Of course, I say the usual things about meeting with students to help them with their writing, but most faculty will never understand what really happens. And perhaps it's best that they don't know. It's okay for colleges to have places of mystery and magic.

It is a place where people get help with almost every stage of writing: not just grammars.

A dream! Students have worked really hard to create the WC—at times it seemed like an impossible goal.

It is a place that offers writing support for everyone.

We are open all day, with teachers on duty. Students, and teachers and administrators, drop in for help with writing.

We help writers through the process of writing and support them as sounding boards while offering resources for writers at all levels. We also provide workshops.

A hub for reading, writing, & thinking.

We tell both students and faculty that we're available to support students when they write, regardless of what kind of writing students do. We tell faculty that we're available to support their own writing and teaching. We do occasionally have to remind faculty that we're not an editing service, although that's more rare, and we try to articulate ways in which we do help students rather than focusing on what we don't do. When students ask for proofreading, we explain how we can help them with sentence-level concerns because most times, students (and even faculty) use the term "proofreading" as a catch-all term. Many time, we simply tell students that we're here to offer feedback.

I believe that my school's writing lab fits my definition of a writing lab perfectly.

Our writing center has helped untold thousands of students to develop their writing skills, especially by discussing rules of grammar (more for ESL students), why certain constructs work (or don't), how to develop a strong thesis, conclusion, supporting paragraphs and transition, to name a few types of coverage. I believe this has led to greater future success of our graduates.

We always begin by saying a writing center is a supplemental resource to reinforce what students learn in class and which provides students with information, materials, and tutors to help with any stage of the writing process for any course. Then we tell people what we do not do (take drop off papers because the student must be there to work on his/her own paper, fix papers, assure an A, etc.).

The writing center's role is to support the writing/speaking/visualizing endeavors of students, faculty, and staff, and to be a hub for writing activities throughout the university.

It is a place for students, faculty, and staff where they can bring any writing assignment, draft, or ideas and receive feedback from a tutor. It is not a fix-it shop.

We serve a large population of Second Language Speakers, so in addition to more normal functions, we really do much of the work of an international student center.

This is the official mission:

The X Writing Center, a center for writers and writing, serves the entire X community with an emphasis on assisting student writers from all X courses. To reflect our mission, we strive to 1) offer numerous writing-related resources to students, staff, and faculty across campus, 2) use interactive conferences to encourage student writers to become more confident, self-aware, and empowered as they participate in academic and other discourse communities, 3) explore and apply innovations in writing center theory to the benefit of writing center patrons, and 4) provide valuable paraprofessional experiences for students who work as peer tutors. Less officially:

To faculty and students, I talk less about what the writing center is and more about what happens there—what does a typical session look like, what have tutors been trained to do, how to come to a session prepared, etc. I also talk to faculty and about how the writing center can help their students. To administrators, I stress the important role the center plays both for writers who use it but also for writers who work as tutors.

To potential tutors, I talk about how the center is a learning community for all those involved and a great one to join.

We serve largely as a polishing shop, although frequently we have to help the writer deconstruct the meaning and make it new again.

I tell them that it is always better for a fresh set of eyes to read someone else's work, at the very least, emphasizing that the tutors are easy to work with and non-judgmental. In addition, I make the point that the writing center is not just for those who struggle with the task but, rather, can be a boon for everyone.

A positive and supportive place where people can work to expand their communication skills with peers.

I "advertise" the center as support for writing in the classroom and as an audience for student work.

I describe myself as a "second set of eyes" that are used to look over a paper. I'm the outside observer—the exterior influence—that is brought in during the writing process to advise and offer feedback.

Unclear question.

Faculty and administration still seem to view it as a place for "struggling" writers—the typical "go get this cleaned up/taken care of" at the writing center. So while I want to talk about the rhetorical function of grammar, I'm expected to reiterate the importance of how to diagram a sentence and write a "clean" 5-para essay.

A support unit for students, a sanctuary for those who have decoded it's mystic, and a mystery for those afraid to engage in full-frontal writing.

It's not a place for "bad writers" but for those who care about their writing.

As a place where writers and tutors learn about language and writing, in a friendly, protected environment.

A place where students can come for one-to-one work on writing issues that trouble them; and a place where instructors can look for support in bringing writing into their courses.

Well, I tell my students that a lot of expertise on academic writing is housed in the WC, and therefore stopping by at any stage of the process is helpful. I generally depict the center as a form of student support services but try to distance it from the stigmas (albeit inaccurate) of tutoring or LD services.

Fits pretty clearly—we all worked to develop this program over the past 10 years and, although we disagree on approaches, all have the same goal of helping students.

We value, support, and mentor writing and writers at every level and in every discipline.

We talk with writers about their processes and texts to help them figure out ways to improve those texts and to help them recognize what they're doing successfully in their writing and to build on that success. We serve as live readers whose immediate reactions can help students recognize how their meaning making efforts are being experienced by a reader.

I'm a business writing consultant, which means that I primarily tutor students with resumes, cover letters, and other business documents. I hope to teach tutees the skills to be able to write or improve these documents themselves.

It is useful for outside input on your paper, in addition to the tips and betterment available. We are also open for any stage of the writing process, including brainstorming and editing.

I described the role of our writing center in the first question. In that question, I included our students as well as people from our community. As a community college, we serve the large and diverse student population that the college has (17,000 students currently) but we also are here to help the community, which is an extremely diverse population.

It is a wac-based writing center where we work with students, faculty, administration, staff and alumni with any aspect of writing from pre-writing to final draft. We tell all that we are not responsible for students' grades because we do not "correct" their papers. We ask questions rather than give answers.

While a few classes requires frequent visits to the writing center, quite a few students drop in for advice in many different fields. We are there to assist in any moment of the writing process, be it brainstorming, drafting, or formatting.

We support writing across the curriculum for all levels of students and in a manner tailored to fit the needs of each individual student. We are committed to seeing each student as an individual, identifying his/her needs, strength, and goals, and the supporting him/her in learning the skills that will help the student independently achieve those aims. In other words, if we do our job right, we put ourselves out of business.

Writing support for all student writers.

When I give Wriring Center Orientations to classes, I try to balance my talk on the "hows" of the sessions (how to sign in, how to make appointments, etc.) along with academic writing in general. I speak about writing broadly.

I help students with their papers, not by writing or editing them, but by engaging them in conversation about their ideas and arguments in order to help them to articulate these in a strong, clear and cohesive paper.

Writing centers provide a safe, open space for writers of all levels to receive support for their writing projects—anything from a personal statement or resume, thesis or dissertation, and the odd hometown newspaper column written for their favorite charity.*

Provides one-on-one assistance to support students as they become better writers.*

This is the wording that I encourage faculty members to use on their syllabi:

The [Name] College Writing Center provides free, one-on-one consultations to all [Name] students. Our tutors have been intensely trained, and while they won't rewrite students' papers for them, they will give students feedback and encouragement at all stages of the writing process (brainstorming, drafting, revising, polishing). Students who use the Writing Center should be prepared to discuss the assignment they are working on and to begin making revisions, with the tutor's guidance, during the session.

All students are encouraged to use the Writing Center which is open afternoons (in ADMN 211) and evenings (in the Library, Study Room #5). Walk-ins are welcome, but the Writing Center honors appointments first. For more information or to make an appointment, call [Name] or stop by ADMN 211.

Since we primarily work with undergrad students, that is how I'd generally describe the work that we do: peer tutors work with other students on their writing.

A place where students can get one-on-one assistance with writing projects of any kind, and a place where students interested in writing can find resources to further and develop their interests.*

Support for language arts instruction in GED preparation classes.

The Writing Center allows students to help students; staffing the Writing Center with student tutors (we call them scribes) makes student writers more comfortable in seeking out help.

As a facility that offers a free service to any member of the community wherein trained consultants will engage participants in conversations to determine and address writing issues.

Because our aim is to produce better writers—not just better writing (North)—our tutors work closely with students to help them acquire for themselves the writing skills they need not only in their classes but in their future careers. Accordingly, tutors do not provide editing or proofreading services; rather, they help students learn how to express themselves clearly and coherently in any writing situation they may encounter. In addition, the Studio offers a range of workshops designed not only for students but also for faculty, staff, and the community.

I always just say that my job is to help students become more comfortable with effectively completing their writing assignments in class so that they may also be more comfortable using writing more generally outside of the classroom. I also define my job as a way to help faculty members (from disciplines outside English) find ways to bring writing pedagogy into their classrooms in an effective way.

The writing center is largely a place to get help on papers, but I'm afraid it might not get publicized enough as a place to develop ideas and is seen as more of a one-stop grammar check place.

I call it "the most important place on campus."

An open area for all those who require addition aid in writing.

The writing center is designed to help in any area of writing or the writing process that a student or professor needs.

I don't know if I understand this question. If it is asking how I explain the work of our writing center to the non-writing center people at our institution, here's an answer: "The writing center isn't here b/c students can't write, it's here b/c they do." (I stole that famous line :) "In the writing center, you sit down and have conversations about your writing—where you're stuck, what your plans are, what your questions are—at any stage of your writing process."

Central. It is used as much by grad students as by undergrads, and supports faculty as well in their writing instruction and curricula. Our W C also administers placement into writing courses, so it has an administrative capacity as well.

Our center will assist you develop writing skills throughout all stages of your writing process—from helping you explore the topic to teaching you proofreading skills.

The writing center functions as a stepping stone to becoming the writer that the student wants to be.

The Writing Center has some very good tutors who can assist with grammar, syntax, and reviewing your paper. They do not edit papers. They also do not provide much "pre-writing" assistance as they are very busy with brief 20 minutes appointments with freshmen comp students . . .

A place where students of any level of academic ability can come to meet with peer tutors in order to improve their writing.

It, at this point, does excellent writing consulting with a small percentage of the whole student body.

If you need help with brainstorming, organization, thesis, or grammar, the peer tutors or professional tutors at the writing center can help you out.

A place where you can go to try and make your papers better, as well as making yourself a better writer.

When I begin tutoring regularly, I will be tutoring for three credits in the Writing Center, and my duty and goal is to help other students with their writing.

The goal is to make better writers. Anyone at any skill point can become a better writer. Not a fix-it shop for grammar.

Our writing center is not as frequently used as I would like it to be, but as it stands, freshmen and sophomores bring their essays to us in hopes that we can give them enough suggestions for them to get a A on their paper.

Question 6. In what ways do you think your writing center is different from other writing centers?

My writing center is not afraid to offer more directive tutoring for students who need it. My tutors even write on students' papers and suggest editing strategies. The horror!

I've worked at three writing centers, all of them when I was a student. I now run the one where I started. This Writing Center is at a two year institution so we see a lot of developmental writers (meaning they haven't passed our profiecency exam), as well as many composition students. No senior thesis papers or graduate students here.

The last couple of years our center was mostly run by grad students, but we'll be getting a new full-time staff director in the fall.

It's a very open-minded place. It's a private arts school, so it's given that it's creative and bright with so many ideas flowing throughout.

I'm not very sure how other writing centers function, so I'm unable to answer.

I only have one other writing lab to compare it to, but I feel that ours has more space for both undergraduate and graduate tutors to work in the same space. It is also the tutors responsibility to help answer emailed questions.

We serve GED students and our staff is all volunteer.

It is part of the university's Learning Studio. This means that students can receive help from all disciplines at a central location.

Due to the fact that our writing center is part of a community college, we work with both students and members of the community. On top of that, both our student population and our community are very diverse culturally with people from all over the worl calling Lake County, "home." With our student population coming from this community, we have an extremely high percentage of ESL and L2 students who struggle with their language, the English language and the interconnection of the two. I do think this is very different from other writing centers that I have visited. In addition, we are a very busy center since we serve so many students and the surrounding area.

We are staffed primarily by writing professionals with advanced degrees who also teach writing in the classroom. A few grad students and peer tutors are chosen each semester, but they must undergo an internship in the writing center before they are allowed to tutor other students.

Our faculty do a significant number of presentations and workshops in classes. Additionally, we are a combined reading/writing center that is responsible for delivering "tier 2" services for students performing below standards in reading/writing. ALL students are mandated to work in our writing center for specific assignments each year.

In very small ways. Other centers seem to have the same primary goal, and they work from higher-order concerns, using open-ended questions. But there are some things we do that other centers might not: admninister the grammar and intermediate writing clep-exams, and work with education students in a skills development process to prepare them for written exam in the teaching education program.

Not having much contact with other writing centers, I think ours is less focused on satisfying professors' wishes and more focused on students' needs (which are sometimes the same but not always). We are small for a school our size.

We allow for professors to require visits. Though we recognize this may create tension, we also believe that if entire classes are required to come see us, it eliminates the perception that going to the writing center is a punishment. It helps us position ourselves as a positive support that professors endorse. And, the required visits give us a chance to have student contact (we're a new center still trying to gain visibility).

Our center is the hub of writing instruction at a highly selective, small liberal arts college that does not have any writing requirements or writing across the curriculum program.

I think our writing center has administrative staff who are committed to educating and developing the writing consultants as much as the whole student body. Therefore, we have more resources (my time, even some cash) devoted to consultant development than at other schools with which I am familiar.

I think we include play and laughter in our work and in our sessions. I also think our staff works collaboratively not just with students, but with each other during sessions and on projects. We socialize outside the center.

We have only professional tutors, mostly adjunct instructors and writing center-dedicated staff who can work up to 20 hours/week. We also collaborate with our school's developmental writing program where one tutor is assigned a class that they visit once/week for one hour and twenty minutes for the entire semester. During these visits, the tutor works with small groups of students to facillitate discussion about the students' writing.

I don't think we are so different; we have a lot in common with many centers. Having said that, some centers report students' visits and what was taught to instructors; we won't. Some others have, necessarily, more emphasis on sentence-level work than we do; our work is primarily with upper-division and graduate students.

I know other writing centers operate like this, but for me it has been a big difference when compared to other writing center's I've been involved with. All of our tutors are graduate students who have to work in the writing center as part of their GA duties. I think that really influences everything we do.

I think we may have more autonomy or independence in setting our policies than other writing centers may face. We have a good deal of institutional support for writing consultants to present at national and regional conferences. Because we are rarely told "no" as a department, our consultants are free to pursue their interests; as a result, we've developed a lot of relationships with other programs and departments on our campus.

Most likely our student body make us different. Being at an open access institution makes a big difference.

It is embedded in an interdisciplinary Comprehensive Learning Center that serves seven core subject areas. Writing, by the way, is the only "subject area" that transcends disciplines, ie we serve writers in every type of course.

I doubt if this is necessarily "diofferent" but what we focus on in teaching skills (rather than just helping a student "get through") and we do that by looking not just at the student's writing but also at the student: what are his/her other learning patterns? is their any reading comprehension issue that is contributing to the written struggles? study skills issues? needs for tools for organizing, categorizing, planning? And because we listen and observe carefully, we also find ourselves addressing the life issues that affect a student in and out of the classroom.

We are quite small, only five tutors for a campus with 5,000 students. In addition, we offer writing center services to students in the Masters and Doctoral programs. In some ways we are old-fashioned in the services we offer, for example, we call a telephone session with tutor/student both looking at an e-mailed paper a "virtual" session. I have learned through experience, that there is a lag in our student's adapation of technology.

Well, perhaps we're unique in that we believe in mystery and magic. Apparently we are unique in terms of our size: a staff of 75 undergraduate consultants for a school of 1,250 students. We are also unique in that most of our staff sign up to join the Writing Center while they are still high school seniors. And we have a variety of unique activities: we roast our own coffee, make our own bread, publish a literary journal, support a variety of volunteer programs on campus, etc.

I think every writing center is different (see ecology idea above). That said, as a community college writing center, one of the dynamics we face is the range of preparation/experience the writers have who come to us. One tutee might have a doctorate from Poland and the next will be someone reading and writing at a 6th grade level. Conversely, we don't see as much discipline-specific writing (no senior theses, etc.) because most students will not fully enter a discipline's discourse until they transfer to a 4-year institution. As a community college center, the turnover for our peer tutors is constant. I have most peer tutors for their second and last year here and then they transfer.

I think that the staff is very well educated and continue to expand their educational goals as far as writing. There isn't one person there that thinks that they know everything and they are continuously trying to expand the knowledge base.

This is difficult to answer as almost all my experience with writing centers has been with my current position. Our practice is primarily face to face and spans a broad scope to respond to the perceived need of the tutee. The primary practice (or at least mine) focuses first on organization, style, and meeting the purpose of the document (most often a specific writing assignment for a student's class). The goal is an effective expression of the the writer's knowledge and position. Grammar, punctuation, and spelling are subsidiary to these goals.

We employ a collaborative pedagogy that emphasizes strengthening writing skills, not individual papers which is different from centers that simply respond directly to what clients request gets worked on.

Well, I haven't started directing it yet (July 1!), but so far I don't think it's very different from WCs in similar universities. Over 60% of the clients are ELL, and that's presented great challenges to current staff. Also, staffing is primarily by English department TAs and undergrad majors. It's very much an "English Department" Writing Center, and my task is to make it a "University" Writing Center.

We serve on walk-in basis (no appointments); we do not limit the length of sessions or numbers of allowable visits; we do only face-to-face sessions. I imagine we would be considered old-fashioned.

Most importantly, we are committed to social justice, anti-racism, universal access, and ending gender and sexuality discrimination through our work. Most writing centers don't seem to take a hard stance on these issues. However, I don't doubt that our work to try to end oppression(s) through our everyday work has resulted in our flourishing on our campus. We are also much more democratically run—all the tutors participate in the hiring process, and all the tutor structure our trainings and help make the big decisions for our center.

It is new—only 3 months old. Currently staffed by English teachers. Hoping to have peer tutors soon.

Unfortunately, we do not have a formal, consistent training program, so I am constantly cobbling together a staff and staff community. We are a "full service" program, so we help any student writer on campus, but we have no training course and our pay is terrible ($9.00 per hour). We hire graduate and undergraduate students, so I have undergraduates who work with Masters and doctoral students. This combination works for us, but it take a lot of energy!

First, being almost solely undergraduates, it differs very much from all graduate, mostly graduate, or professional tutor centers. Then, amongst all (or virtually all) undergraduate tutors (I have one grad student each year), I think, like I mentioned above, we are becoming more holistic, seeing the critical importance of the affective element in improving students as writers.

We place more emphasis on tutees as peers, rather than a teacher/ student relationship.

Possibly an ever-present emphasis on the essential but differently-situated expertise of the collaborators as well as a commitment to the director being one of those collaborators.

We're smaller, which gives us more time to work with writers.

I am not sure that it is much different from other secondary school writing centers in my state.

Nothin in particular comes to mind. Few points of comparison. I guess we, as both staff and in student body, are very hegemonic.

It seems to be a lot better funded and respected than the people who write about writing centers are.

I think that although they SAY that they do not edit—in the end, they just edit. They might not actually take the paper and edit the paper—but they really only have time to hit a few of the lower order concerns that student's present. When a student comes in with higher order issues it's like they ignore them or don't see them. They don't feel confident enough to question the writer about their organization or structure or their level of detail??? I feel like other Writing Centers might do this better.

It's much more student-centered and consistent in following the higher order to lower order concerns.

We don't have any peer tutors; we have what we call professional tutors . . . people with Master's degrees in a writing-related field who have previous experience as instructors and/or tutors. We also tutor graduate students, faculty and staff. We also do mostly drop-in consults, not appointments.

I don't know that we are that different from most, either in location, funding, status and use.

Our center is different from other centers on campus in that we will not provide line edits; we help clients identify individual patterns, discuss the impact of that error pattern on the writing sample, and work through some revisions with the client. Our center is different from centers at other campuses because we are funded by the English Department, although our mission is to serve the campus community which includes 10 external campuses in addition to the 50,000 students, faculty, and staff at our main campus—with 10 consultants working 10 hours a week.

I don't know. I haven't really researched any other writing centers.

Because I'm at a 2 year career college, most students are not getting a liberal arts education. They want their degree to be a radiological technologist or an occupational therapist assistant but don't see writing as a tool to help them achieve those goals. This attitude is not unusual, but these particular students are less prepared than at traditional universities and the instructors often do not have terminal degrees, so many of them also don't see the point. It's a much different environment from a traditional school.

Push strategy for us vs. pull strategy for others.

I think my writing center is different in that it is not directly associate with any particular department. It is currently a part of the Undergraduate Tutorial Center, which has it's pros and cons. Ultimately though, I think this could be a good position for the center.

We may be different in that we extensively train and nationally certify our tutors.

We have a schedule outside of our writing center for students to schedule appointments. I'm not familiar with other writing centers, but I'm assuming some of them are walk-in.

We serve more students because we are well-funded and have imbedded tutors in our writing-intensive courses.

We have a very small staff of tutors (about 6 GAs each semester) who must be available for the 20,000 + people in the university community.

The director has no say in which graduate students become tutors. Roughly 70% of clients are multilinguals whose first language is not English. Thus, tutors are specially trained to work with the university's culturally and linguistically diverse population.

We include public speaking and are the locus for a campus-wide writing-in-the-disciplines programs. That does not make us unique, but not many centers do this. We employ tutors from all disciplines, graduate, undergraduate, and professional, some international, too, and we serve graduate and undergraduate and do faculty development.

I feel our leadership is unique in their support of tutors and encouragement of research, confrences, and personal growth in the tutors. We are not as well funded as other writing centers, which greatly limits our space and our staff.

I'm sure there is a lot of difference, as I've noticed quite a bit from when I was a peer tutor at a 4-year private liberal arts school, a grad tutor at a R1 school, and now a "professional" tutor at an open admissions community college. I have an idealized version of writing centers: they're "talking back" to faculty who focus narrowly on proficiency, providing a vibrant space for the writing community on their campus, getting students excited about writing. Where I am now there is a lot of focus on proficiency, which I find frustrating and stifling.

We enjoy a long history than many writing centers, and we also have an interesting mix of graduate and undergraduate tutors. Our undergraduate tutors serve in specialized roles. We're also able to provide more administrative positions and professional development opportunities to our tutors than some centers. Unlike some centers, we are still physically and financially situated within the English department.

Not sure.

The focus on campus-wide connections and collaboration.

Well, we do allow for more discussion of grammar than some writing centers—many of our clients are early writers. We also see a high volume of students since we are a walk-in service (2500–3000 sessions per semester). We have also formed partnerships with the ESL program, developmental learning teachers, and career transitions. These features surely overlap with some writing centers, but I feel these partnerships also make us unique compared to some.

We have abandoned many practices that were standard for years, such as maintaining detailed records of tutorials. We use few handouts or "tip sheets." We involve tutors in all aspects of planning, developing materials and policies and procedures. We focus most public relations efforts on students directly, though we are generally cordial to faculty. We have drastically reduced workshops because they are not cost-effective for a modest staff at a large university.

I think we have very close and friendly relationships not just with each other, but with our supervisors. I have never occupied a position where I have felt so welcome and joyed as I have as a writing tutor.

I'm not sure how common this is, but our writing center has tutors from the faculty as well as peer tutors. It's well-respected by professors.

We have many students who work with other students.

I don't have much experience with other writing centers, but peer tutors are required to reflect on their strategies through weekly journals which allows the tutor to learn from the student just as much as the student learns from the tutor.

We employ mostly professional consultants who work full-time of consulting and generating handouts/workshops.

The biggest difference I think is that we are so busy that we don't market to the campus at all. Another difference is that we do not tutor online—yet.

[Name] College is an art school, so many of the writing assignments brought to the writing center are creative in nature. Our building is set up with artistic, aesthetic and acoustic principles in mind and it creates a colorful, welcoming flow.

I really can't answer this question because I'm simply not familiar enough with what occurs at other centers.

Currently, tutors are recruited from two specific colleges (Honors, International Studies), and there is not an open method of having students from any major or college apply for tutoring positions. Also, this campus lacks a credit-bearing course on the teaching of writing (for tutors, ed specialists, etc.) Finally, no online options available.

We have both full time, well paid faculty—who conduct tutoring sessions as well as teaching writing courses—and an undergrad staffed peer tutoring center, whose tutors are trained, rigorously, by some of our faculty. Faculty also have opportunities to conduct research, speak at conferences, etc.

Although we're all lecturers, we are accorded a different respect and responsibility than lecturers in almost any other department or unit at the University.

Because our university is predominantly a business-focused university, we probably need to support students with some different genres of writing than those at other universities. One of the major ways I think our center is unique is that there is no writing curriculum at our university. This leads to us seeing different types of writing from students, and to students and faculty perhaps viewing us differently?

We are located in a Seminary with a large population of international students, so both the paper assignments we receive and the proportion of international students who visit are Writing Center are different from the "typical" Writing Center.

Solely peer tutoring—there are no faculty/administrative tutors.

We're big—it's a big university. We have three sets of tutors. And we provide substantial pre-service and in-service training (don't like that word) for all staffs. We have a graduate seminar in writing center admininstration as well as practica for tutors, and conisderable research is conducted here. I place a lot less emphasis on tutors' avoiding direct instruction than many other WCDs (I think), and I really care about language level-issues, so I avoid the HOCs?LOCs distintion in preparing tutors.

We have only two professional tutors staffing our center, so we are much smaller than almost every other writing center and we do assist students with lower-order concerns, unlike some other writing centers.

We are an exclusively online writing center. While we definitely have company and colleagues in this arena, we are in a unique situation since we work for a for-profit 4-year online university. Sometimes I feel isolated by public and private learning institutions at conferences like the IWCA Collaborative because many of my colleagues do not see me or my writing center colleagues as reputable writing center practitioners despite our education and experiences in many other writing centers (public, private, and two-year community colleges). I think our writing center and our staff have a lot to share with private and public writing center colleagues about how to leverage online tutoring in a meaningful and thoughtful way for students and writing center staff. We truly want to share and learn from others' scholarship.

Our WC, in a high school, was brought into existence by a class of students who worked all year to educate themselves about WCs and advocated with their principal and other staff to create a WC.

We look like a grammar lab but we use the grammar software that the teachers assign their students to do in our center as a nexus for them to see that all writers need help and the help they will recieve from us is friendly/accessible.

It is smaller, in both space and numbers of tutors. We are well funded—our problems aren't caused by a lack of funds. We sometimes have trouble recruiting tutors even though the pay is good, relatively speaking.

We welcome faculty, staff, and students to use our writing center; our primary tutors are full time professionals with backgrounds as peer tutors from other centers; about a fifth of our weekly tutoring hours are from faculty volunteers.

It is not a remedial facility; it is for all students, staff, faculty, alumni, administrators, and parents.

Unfortunately, we are only available one out of seven periods. Our hope is to grow into a center where we have tutors available to help students in all academic areas—as a literacy center.

Our hours, probably. I've heard of writing centers opening at 7 in the morning, but we only work 1–4 and 7–10 on most days. Also, I think the word choice our center uses by calling the tutors "consultants" is different. A lot of places use the word "tutor," which implies a less equal relationship, it seems like.

It's small. Because our college has only 1000 students, I can only really justify a staff of about 5–7 tutors. We're staffed only by undergraduates. I model the center I direct on the center I tutored in as an undergraduate, so I don't think it's totally unique in anyway. If anything, I try to justify that our writing center is "just like" centers on other campuses.

We are always having workshops, role-playing, and discussions about how to improve our work at the Writing Center. The staff meetings that we have every other week help immensely because we can share our triumphs and challenges as tutors, and learn how to support each other. Our Writing Center also fosters students' and faculty's creativity, because we have resources such as magnetic poetry, and humorous posters that make people feel comfortable and welcome. We also focus on working with the student in a collaborative approach, rather than take a directive approach where the tutor is more engaged than the student.

Well, I love the collegiality at this writing center. There's a focus on professional development/improving practice. There's also a focus on care—of consultant and of consultees.

It has been in operation at our school for almost 25 years. It is student staffed and the student director(s) are responsible for most of the organizational elements of its operation.

It's within our learning center and located in an excellent facility on the first floor of our library. Five years ago it was in a dilapidated house on the edge of campus. We moved to better space five years ago and then last year got a nice remodel. So our institution is giving our learning center a higher budget priority, not lower, in recent years.

Not sure. One thing I believe distinguishes ours is the center's commitment to supplant the education experience of English majors and Education majors. Our grad students and highly-placed undergrads receive a lot of attention and are urged to develop scholarship based on their experience and perceptions.

I am a relatively new staff member, therefore I do not know much about other writing centers. However, I do know my writing center offers group workshops delivered in classrooms, writing center tours for freshmen, satellite locations during evening hours to accommodate students with full schedules during the daytime hours, and three types of tutors: graduate tutors (English doctoral students), undergrad tutors (who take a year-long course to tutor freshman English), and business writing consultants (who take a year-long course to tutor students' and staff resumes, cover letters, memos, and other business-type writing)

We have a lot of resources for students, including online conferences, and we are usually available to help students when they need help. Other centers seem more restrained because of a lack of resources.

We take two courses prior to becoming a full tutor and the center doesn't allow graduate students to be tutors.

Foreign language tutoring. Online tutoring.

We are housed with other centers for science, math, foreign language, and supplemental instruction. We also are in the middle of several special projects including tutoring mentorship and imbedded tutoring.

I think our writing center is different because of the passion and excitement we all put into our work. Everyone gets along incredibly well, and each person has their own specialization. If I come across a student with a long-term specific need, I never hesitate to refer them to one of our outstanding "in-house experts." There is no feeling of competition or inadequacy among our group because of the honesty we share on our staff blog and in our staff meetings. We all have struggling sessions; we all have rockstar moments. It is great to learn from each other and work toward the goal of improving as a team, not just as an individual tutor.

Length of tutor training—we are trained for over an entire semester.

We are more "comprehensive" in that we house WAC programs, a National Writing Project site, a research grants program, and a graduate student minor.

Our center is staffed entirely by student Writing Advisors. They are trained to run conferences with other students on writing. Faculty do not run conferences, and we do not provide computer facilities or work space for anything but one-on-one conferencing. We also run a visiting writers series that brings professionals to campus throughout the school year.

Question 7. In what ways do you think your writing center is similar to other writing centers?

We provide a welcoming, friendly, supportive environment for student-writers.

We all have the same "idea" of what a writing center is. But now that I'm thinking about it, the private, 4-year college I transfered to and worked at for 2 years was much more concerned with the "correctness" of papers and reports. We used to have weekly meetings where the Coordinator used to go over our reports and correct our wording to make it more concise. Used to drive us mad! And I liked to report about the students' writing process in the reports, but the Coordinator insis-ited that "instructors don't care about their students' writing process." I'd argue with her that they did. However, though I continued to talk about process to students, I stopped writing about that in the reports.

We all tout our roles as not being those of copy-editors.:)

We all break it down to the same goal: to have students leaving ful-filled, more knowledgeable, and have a better understanding of the writ-ing process and/or how it pertains to their assignment.

I think that all around most writing centers have the same goal, which is to generally help the students who seek help.

I think they are similar in services provided, with tutoring both strictly academic papers and business documents.

Tutors and students work together on writing and writing processes.

It works toward the same goals as other writing centers, has similar training, etc.

I have only visited 2 other writing centers, but at these other centers I felt that their main goal was similar to ours in making the students feel comfortable to engage in conversation about their paper. In each case, the tutors took time with their students to get them to open up about their writing and delve into the underlying meanings. We too strive to do this rather than to simply skim the surface.

The ultimate goal—finding a way to produce Stephen North's "bet-ter writers."

Student tutors utilize a nondirective approach for working with writ-ers from across the curriculum. Students may make appointments with individual tutors.

See above.

We love helping students with writing. I think our goals line up with other writing centers (to help students become better writers), we just go about it differently.

We try to keep tutoring fairly non-directive (though we sometimes are probably more directive than other centers). We also try to maintain a warm atmosphere, and we try to provide opportunities to peer tutors that will allow them to use their position as good resume material for grad school applications (resource development, conference presentations, etc.)

similar in mission of collaboration, conversation, and sustained peer learning.

Most writing centers engaged with other writing centers share a deep commitment to serving all writers, not only those deemed in need of remediation.

I hope that we are similar in our dedication to helping people become more confident communicators.

We try to work on higher order concerns before lower order concerns (depending on when the student's assignment is due); we focus on building relationships with our stakeholders; we work through misconceptions students and faculty have about our work.

Common missions, theories, and pedagogy. High standards for consultants.

we provide multiple avenues for tutoring (online, face-to-face, drop-ins at a library location). we have 50 minute sessions. we tutor one-to-one.

One-on-one peer-tutoring sessions are at the heart of what we do. As a four-year college, we have students cycling in and out all the time, so it's an ongoing challenge to make sure that we articulate our mission to new students; recruiting and educating new consultants is also an ongoing challenge.

I think writing centers have far more in common than they have differences. working with students one-to-one, of course is the major similarity.

Training, staffing, philosophy are all mainstream. We work a lot with developmental and non-native writers . . . we fight admin and budget cuts. We do not (yet) offer online conferencing. I attend CCCC's, IWCA, NCPTW.

We want to empower students

We are like other writing centers in our effort to move student/professor attention to higher order concerns; we spend a great deal of time on documentation styles to our dismay; and almost all of our tutors, as well as I take our mission and our work very seriously. We like most other writing centers feel as if we are doing important work.

We try to help students become better students, to experience the benefits of working with their peers, to engage in interesting and thought-provoking conversations, and occasionally to help students produce better papers.

I think we are similar in our approach to handling the tension between indirect/direct tutoring—that is, tutors need to negotiate that continuum with every student they work with. Though we do lots of PR, we constantly have to educate faculty and students about what it is we do and don't do (as well as remind them of the complexity of writing as a process). We see a lot of second language writers. These are issues that I think are common to most writing centers. I'm sure there are other ways that we are similar but those are the ones that first came to mind.

I don't think that it is similar at all. The people that work there are friendly and very knowledgeable and don't treat you like you don't matter.

- broad cross-section of writers
- significant ELL poplulation
- 30–50 minute visits
- some users are frequent visitors

I think that our center is similar to others in that we engage in current pedagogy and promote tutors to become professionally active. We also see a lot of International Students just as I have heard other centers do.

I think I just answered that above!

All consultants are students (both undergraduate and graduate). All consultants are writers themselves—mostly but not all English majors.

We utilize peer tutors, tutor writing, and follow many of the same tenants of other writing centers.

Open to drop in appointments, mission is to improve student writing and comfort level with themselves as writers.

We use conversation to help writers discover their rhetorical needs and improve their writing. We work with a wide variety of writers and are the only place on campus that offer help to doctoral students working on dissertations, students with disabilities, students who do not speak

English as a first language, and developmental writers. We are still misunderstood by many faculty (but not most faculty) who see us as an extension of their classrooms and therefore in lesser, remedial positions. Once a semester or so a faculty member lets me know a student who visited the Writing Center still had mechanical issues.

We love working with students, we focus on the student more than the text, we encourage, we teach and model, we laugh and talk, we enjoy being with each other.

well, our focus is on helping people with writing

serious commitment to writers and writing

We believe in writing as a process that allows for constructive interventions on the way to a finished product, i.e., the text.

Collaborative, conversational, supportive,

Practice. Like a lot of other education systems/constructs share a lot of their information, strategies and findings. Since we use guidance material from sources common in the field, I would guess a lot of theory and practice is similar.

I'm sure we work on a lot of the same things with the people who come in: transitions, grammar, thesis statements, that kind of stuff.

I don't know.

It focuses on building better writers, and its success is closely linked the the tenacity and charisma of the director. When he retires, I worry what will become of this 25+ year success story.

In most ways, really. We share frustrations when students/faculty think we are fix-it shops, and, similarly, we share successes when students and tutors accomplish much . . . and eventually the student doesn't need us: he/she has become a more confident writer.

See the answer above.

We are becoming more like other 21st century writing centers as we struggle to change the perception of the center from fix-it shop to "CENTER FOR WRITING EXCELLENCE."

I suppose we all seek to improve the writing of others. Aside from that, please see previous question.

We all want to see our students' confidence built as they learn to tackle more and more difficult writing tasks and (from what I understand) we all want to focus on the bigger concerns (organization, transitions, source integration) rather than the smaller concerns (commas, formatting). Most other ways.

I employ peer consultants to work with writers, and we follow common best practices in the field.

We're very similar because we've taken parts of The University of [Name] Writing Center, [Name] Writing Center, [Name] WC, and others.

We are run by students (juniors and seniors) and we give other students a second opinion on their writing.

offer one-on-one sessions

We are learner- and learning-centered. Therefore, we don't engage in grade-based discussions. We do not proofread/edit, but we assist learners in learning to do it on their own. We fight uphill battles against uninformed faculty who send their students to the WC to get their writing ""fixed"" because the student's ""grammar is bad."

We stress individualized instruction and active learning, collaboration, and talking, one-on-one.

We work with writers. We go to conferences. We have the same basic structure of a director(s) and tutors. Many of our tutors are graduate students.

My guess is that all writing centers feel the pressure to "teach" the basics of writing to those who exhibit any kind of difference: the underprepared, ESL, etc.

We spend time training our tutors to use minimalist tutoring strategies and to consider HOCS first, although each student's context may determine the course of a tutorial session. We're happy to engage with different parts of campus to support discipline-specific writing needs. We have a positive reputation on campus.

the kind of help provided with the writing process—even if our exact procedures are different from theirs

our attempt to put writing on the agenda, the focus on the process. our use of peer consultants, the training of them.

We focus primarily on higher order concerns in tutoring sessions, and we encourage students to assume control over tutoring sessions. We conduct a workshop series each semester that covers several issues in academic writing, such as citation styles, types of argumentative writing, and recognizing rhetoric. We also field many misguided requests from faculty and students ("my students using the center are not getting As—fix that"), and we frequently have to remind our college community of our mission.

We use peer tutors. We are about writing. We spend time in classrooms talking about the writing center.

We provide students a service that often they would not be able to receive solely from a Professor or a Teaching Assistant. They can openly discuss their writing and thought process without feeling the constant strain of communicating with some who will be grading them. We occupy an important middle ground, or shelter if you will.

Similar philosophies. "Not a fix-it shop."

It is still advertised as a place to "fix" mistakes in papers.

We engage in individualized consultations to identify individual writing/communication/rhetorical issues on a case-by-case basis and work with clients to develop strategies to cope with those issues.

Our tutoring is similar to most writing centers—flexible and student-centered.

We offer one-on-one tutoring. Writers and tutors meet in cubicles that divide a large room into smaller sections.

Same response as the previous one.

Mission statement, undergraduate and graduate tutors from student body, tutor praxis (standards, conversational methods approach), challenges of space and place, budgetary challenges, having teachers understand what we do, getting teachers to recommend the writing center as a place for writers of all levels

Our pedagogy, our open-mindedness.

We work on the process of writing, we work with students at all stages of the writing proecess, we view the writing tutorial session as a learning experience for both the writer and the writing consultant

We struggle with the same issues: professors and students who would like us to be a proofreading service, tutors who offer differing degrees of help.

Study of WC theory.

We all love working with students and with each other, and work to maintain it as a happy place.

We are similar in that we let students lead the way most of the time, we do not proofread, we have individual sessions, we are nonthreatening, and we are flexible.

We have an online reference library replete with podcasts, videos, handouts, a Facebook page, and Twitter feed; we participate and present at the EWCA, IWCA, regional writing center associations like the MWCA and SCWA, CCCC, NCTE, and WPA, to name a few; we prioritize the students first in our mission and actions; we serve as liaisons between our faculty and students; we help students navigate academic and formal writing contexts; we conduct outreach and online writing workshops (live and recorded) for students and faculty; we're constantly considering how to best serve the needs of our learning community and stakeholders; and we want to inspire confidence, playfulness, and passion in writing.

I think we share a similar philosophy with lots of other WCs about helping create better writers, rather than focusing on simply helping produce better texts.

We provide one on one feedback and support

We are misunderstood. For example, we don't copyedit student papers, although many people (apparently including my dean) think we do. We also don't ghost write student papers. Also, this is hard work!

Dedication to helping those who want to work on their writing do so successfully.

Focus on mentoring, use of writing fellows as well as tutors and professionals.

We use the theory of active listening, we have text resources, we train tutors, we promote literacy.

I don't know enough to say.

See question above. I hope my writing center is very "mainstream." My colleagues think I'm strange enough (young, midwesterner on a very old, very southern faculty) so I try to align my pedagogy and vision of the writing center with what I believe are very widely held practices.

We offer writing resources to students such as formatting and grammar guides, our staff is made up of strong writers, and we work primarily with university affiliates.

The practice of meeting with writers to help with writing.

Our Writing Center focuses on having conversations about writing, on helping writers improve and grow rather than simply improving a paper.

It's set up as an informal atmosphere with physical spaces that encourage collaborative learning.

We provide the basic services found in most all centers, including a computer lab for students to work on what was suggested.

Our mission statement reflects on making writers better instead of merely fixing surface mistakes.

Peer tutoring. 1 to 1 tutoring.

In most instances, the tutors are peers of the writers. We are trained with similar writing center theory.

I think our writing center is similar in our ultimate goal: help student writers become better . . . writers!

We all have the goals.

We do the same core work of one-to-one writing consultation, training a population of undergraduate and graduate student writing consultants using some of the mainstay publications in writing center practice and pedagogy.

We believe in the importance of individual assistance, and we believe firmly that all writers, no matter their level of competence or experience, benefit from objective feedback.

REFERENCES

Abrams, Elizabeth. 1994. "Fear and Loathing in the Videotaping Room, or You Oughta Be in Pictures." In *When Tutor Meets Student*, ed. Martha Maxwell, 117–120. Ann Arbor: University of Michigan Press.

Adams, Katherine, and John L. Adams. 1994. "The Creative Writing Workshop and the Writing Center." In *Intersections: Theory-Practice in the Writing Center*, ed. Joan Mullin and Ray Wallace, 19–24. Urbana, IL: National Council of Teachers of English.

Adler-Kassner, Linda. 2008. *The Activist WPA: Changing Stories About Writers and Writing*. Logan: Utah State University Press.

Balester, Valerie, and James McDonald. 2001. "A View of Status and Working Conditions: Relations between Writing Program and Writing Center Directors." *WPA: Writing Program Administration* 24 (3): 59–82.

Balester, Nancy, Nancy Grimm, Jackie Grutsch McKinney, Sohui Lee, David Sheridan, and Naomi Silver. 2012. "The Idea of a Multiliteracy Center: Six Responses." *Praxis: A Writing Center Journal* 9 (2): NP.

Barnett, Robert, and Lois Rosen. 2008. "The WAC/Writing Center Partnership." In *Writing Centers and Writing across the Curriculum Programs*, ed. Robert Barnett and Jacob Blumner, 1–12. Westport, CT: Greenwood Press.

Bartholomae, David. 1985. "Inventing the University." In *When a Writer Can't Write; Studies in Writer's Block and Other Composing-Process Problems*, ed. Mike Rose, 273–85. New York: Guilford.

Berlin, James A. 1992. "Poststructuralism, Cultural Studies, and the Composition Classroom: Postmodern Theory in Practice." *Rhetoric Review* 11 (1): 16–33. http://dx.doi.org/10.1080/07350199209388984.

Bloom, Lynn. 1997. "Subverting the Academic Master Plot." In *Narration as Knowledge*, ed. Joseph Trimmer, 116–26. Portsmouth, NH: Heinemann.

Boquet, Elizabeth H. 1999. "'Our Little Secret': A History of Writing Centers Pre- to Post-Open Admissions." *College Composition and Communication* 50 (3): 463–82. http://dx.doi.org/10.2307/358861.

Boquet, Elizabeth H. 2002. *Noise from the Writing Center*. Logan: Utah State University Press.

Briggs, Lynn Craigue, and Meg Woolbright, eds. 2000. *Stories from the Center: Connecting Narrative and Theory in the Writing Center*. Urbana, IL: National Council of Teachers of English.

Bruffee, Kenneth. 1984. "Collaborative Learning and the 'Conversation of Mankind.'" *College English* 46 (7): 635–52. http://dx.doi.org/10.2307/376924.

Bruner, Jerome. 1987. *Actual Minds*. Cambridge, MA: Harvard University Press.

Bruner, Jerome. 1990. *Acts of Meaning*. Cambridge, MA: Harvard University Press.

Bruner, Jerome. 1991a. "Self-Making and World-Making." *Journal of Aesthetic Education* 25 (1): 67–78. http://dx.doi.org/10.2307/3333092.

Bruner, Jerome. 1991b. "The Narrative Construction of Reality." *Critical Inquiry* 18 (1): 1–21. http://dx.doi.org/10.1086/448619.

Bruner, Jerome. 2004. "Life as Narrative." *Social Research: An International Quarterly* 71 (3): 691–710.

Carino, Peter. 1995a. "Early Writing Centers: Toward a History." *Writing Center Journal* 15 (2): 103–15.

Carino, Peter. 1995b. "Theorizing the Writing Center: An Uneasy Task." *Dialogue: A Journal for Writing Specialists* 2 (1): 23–37.

Carpenter, Rusty. 2008. "Consultations without Bodies: Technology, Virtual Space, and the Writing Center." *Praxis: A Writing Center Journal* 6 (1): np.

Carroll, Meg. 2008. "Identities in Dialogue: Patterns in the Chaos." *Writing Center Journal* 28 (1): 43–62.

Charlton, Jonikka. 2009. "The Future of WPA Professionalization: A 2007 Survey." *Praxis: A Writing Center Journal* 7 (1): np.

Childers, Pamela. 2011. "Getting beyond Mediocrity: The Secondary School Writing Center as Change Agent." In *Before and After the Tutorial*, ed. Nicholas Mauriello, William Macauley, and Robert Koch, 179–202. Cresskill, NJ: Hampton.

Clark, Irene L. 1990. "Maintaining Chaos in the Writing Center: A Critical Perspective on Writing Center Dogma." *Writing Center Journal* 11 (1): 81–93.

Colpo, Michael, Shawn Fullmer, and Brad E. Lucas. 2000. "Emerging (Web)sites for Writing Centers: Practicality, Usage, and Multiple Voices Under Construction." In *Taking Flight with OWLs: Examining Electronic Writing Center Work*, ed. James Inman and Donna N. Sewell, 75–84. Mahwah, NJ: Erlbaum.

Connolly, Colleen, Amy DeJarlais, Alice Gillam, and Laura Micciche. 1998. "Erika and the Fish Lamps: Writing and Reading the Local Scene." In *Weaving Knowledge Together: Writing Centers and Collaboration*, ed. Carol Peterson Haviland, Maria Notarangelo, Lene Whitely-Putz, and Thia Wolf, 14–27. Emmitsburg, MD: NWCA Press.

Coogan, David. 1999. *The Electronic Writing Center.* Stamford, CT: Ablex.

Cooper, Marilyn. 1994. "Really Useful Knowledge: A Cultural Studies Model for Writing Centers." *Writing Center Journal* 14 (2): 94–7.

Cresswell, Tim. 1996. *In Place, Out of Place: Geography, Ideology, and Transgression.* Minneapolis: University of Minnesota Press.

Crosby, Ben. 2006. "The Benefits of a For-Credit Training Course in Starting and Running a University Writing Center." *Writing Lab Newsletter* 30 (9): 1–5.

Daniell, Beth. 1999. "Narratives of Literacy: Connecting Composition to Culture." *College Composition and Communication* 50 (3): 393–410. http://dx.doi.org/10.2307/358858.

Davis, Kevin. 1995. "Life Outside the Boundary." *Writing Lab Newsletter* 20 (2): 5–7.

Denny, Harry. 2010. *Facing the Center: Toward an Identity Politics of One-to-One Mentoring.* Logan: Utah State University Press.

Doe, Sue. 2011. "Toward a Visible Alliance between Writing Centers and Contingent Faculty: A Social Materialist Approach." In *Before and After the Tutorial*, ed. Nicholas Mauriello, William Macauley, and Robert Koch, 29–52. Cresskill, NJ: Hampton.

Dvorak, Kevin. 2004. "Creative Writing Workshops for ESL Writers." In *ESL Writers*, ed. Shanti Bruce and Bennett A. Rafoth, 39–50. Portsmouth, NH: Boynton/Cook.

Ede, Lisa. 1989. "Writing as Social Process: A Theoretical Foundation for Writing Centers?" *Writing Center Journal* 9 (2): 3–15.

Edwards, Betty. 1999. *The New Drawing on the Right Side of the Brain.* New York: Tarcher/Putnum.

England, Christina. 2005. To WCENTER discussion list, January 26.

Eodice, Michele. 2009. "Will the Rain Follow the Plow?" Paper presented at the annual WPA Conference, Minneapolis, MN, July 16–19.

Eubanks, Philip. 2004. "Poetics and Narrativity: How Texts Tell Stories." In *What Writing Does and How It Does It*, ed. Charles Bazerman and Paul Prior, 33–56. Mahwah, NJ: Lawrence Erlbaum.

Faber, Brenton D. 2002. *Community Action and Organizational Change: Image, Narrative, Identity.* Carbondale: Southern Illinois University Press.

Fishman, Pamela M. 1978. "What Do Couples Talk about When They're Alone?" In *Women's Language and Style*, ed. Douglas Butturff, 11–22. Akron, OH: Department of English, University of Akron.

Fishman, Teddi. 2010. "When It Isn't Even on the Page." In *Multiliteracy Centers*, ed. David Sheridan and James Inman, 59–73. Cresskill, NJ: Hampton Press.

Fleckenstein, Kris. 2010. *Vision, Rhetoric, and Social Action in the Composition Classroom.* Carbondale: Southern Illinois University Press.

Gardner, Clint. 2005. To WCENTER discussion list, January 26.

Gardner, Phillip, and William Ramsey. 2005. "The Polyvalent Mission of Writing Centers." *Writing Center Journal* 25 (1): 25–42.

Geller, Anne Ellen, Michele Eodice, Frankie Condon, Meg Carroll, and Elizabeth Boquet. 2007. *The Everyday Writing Center.* Logan: Utah State University Press.

George, Diana, and Nancy Maloney Grimm. 1990. "Expanded Roles/Expanded Responsibilities: The Changing Nature of Writing Centers Today." *Writing Center Journal* 11 (1): 59–67.

Gillespie, Paul, and Neal Lerner. 2007. *The Longman Guide to Peer Tutoring.* 2nd ed. New York: Pearson/Longman.

Grabill, Jeff, William Hart-Davidson, Stacey Pigg, Paul Curran, Mike McLeod, Jessie Moore, Paula Rosinski, Tim Peeples, Suzanne Rumsey, Martine Courant Rife, Robyn Tasaka, Dundee Lackey, and Beth Brunk-Chavez. 2010. "The Writing Lives of College Students." East Lansing, MI: Writing in Digital Environments Research Center. http://digitalis.nwp.org/sites/default/files/files/119/WIDE_2010_writinglives_whitepaper.pdf.

Grimm, Nancy. 1992. "Contesting the Idea of a Writing Center: Politics of Writing Center Research." *Writing Lab Newsletter* 17 (1): 5–7.

Grimm, Nancy. 1996a. "Rearticulating the Work of the Writing Center." *College Composition and Communication* 47 (4): 523–48. http://dx.doi.org/10.2307/358600.

Grimm, Nancy. 1996b. "The Regulatory Role of the Writing Center: Coming to Terms with a Loss of Innocence." *Writing Center Journal* 17 (1): 5–30.

Grimm, Nancy. 1999. *Good Intentions: Writing Center Work for Postmodern Times.* Portsmouth, NH: Boyton/Cook.

Grimm, Nancy. 2008. "Attending to the Conceptual Change Potential of Writing Center Narratives." *Writing Center Journal* 28 (1): 3–12.

Grimm, Nancy. 2011. "Rethinking Writing Center Work to Transform a System of Advantage Based on Race." In *Writing Centers and the New Racism*, ed. Laura Greenfield and Karen Rowan, 75–100. Logan: Utah State University Press.

Grutsch McKinney, Jackie. 2005. "Leaving Home Sweet Home: Towards Critical Readings of Writing Center Spaces." *Writing Center Journal* 25 (2): 6–20.

Grutsch McKinney, Jackie. 2009. "New Media Matters: Tutoring in the Late Age of Print." *Writing Center Journal* 29 (2): 28–51.

Grutsch McKinney, Jackie. 2010. "New Media (R)evolution: Multiple Models for Multiliteracies." In *Multiliteracy Centers: Writing Center Work, New Media, and Multimodal Rhetoric*, ed. David Sheridan and James Inman, 207–23. New York: Hampton Press.

Hadfield, Leslie, Joyce Kinkead, Tom Peterson, Stephanie Ray, and Sarah Preston. 2003. "An Ideal Writing Center: Re-Imagining Space and Design." In *The Center Will Hold*, ed. Michael Pemberton and Joyce Kinkead, 166–76. Logan: Utah State University Press.

Harris, Muriel. 1986. *Teaching One-to-One.* Urbana, IL: National Council of Teachers of English.

Harris, Muriel. 1988. "SLATE Statement: The Concept of a Writing Center." Urbana, IL: National Council of Teachers of English. Rpt. on International Writing Center Association website. http://writingcenters.org/resources/writing-center-concept/.

Harris, Muriel. 1993. "A Multiservice Writing Lab in a Multiversity." In *Writing Centers in Context*, ed. Joyce Kinkead and Jeanette Harris, 1–27. Urbana, IL: National Council of Teachers of English.

Harris, Muriel. 1997. "Presenting Writing Center Scholarship: Issues for Faculty and Personnel Committees." In *Academic Advancement in Composition Studies*, ed. Richard Gebhardt and Barbara Smith Gebhardt, 87–102. Mahwah, NJ: Erlbaum.

Harris, Muriel. 1999. "Diverse Research Methodologies at Work for Diverse Audiences: Shaping the Writing Center to the Institution." In *The Writing Program Administrator as Researcher*, ed. Shirley Rose and Irwin Weiser, 1–17. Portsmouth, NH: Boynton/Cook.

Harris, Muriel. 2007. "Writing Ourselves into Writing Instruction: Beyond Sound Bytes, Tours, Reports, Orientations, and Brochures." In *Marginal Words, Marginal Works: Tutoring the Academy in the Work of Writing Centers*, ed. William Macauley and Nicholas Mauriello, 75–84. New York: Hampton Press.

Harris, Muriel. 2011. "Foreword: Leaping (Cautiously) into the Future of Writing Centers." In *Before and After the Tutorial*, ed. Nicholas Mauriello, William Macauley, and Robert Koch, ix–xii. Cresskill, NJ: Hampton.

Haswell, Richard H., and Min-Zhan Lu, eds. 2007. *Comp Tales: An Introduction to College Composition through Its Stories*. White Plains, NY: Longman.

Hawthorne, Joan. 2006. "Approaching Assessment as If It Matters." In *Writing Center Director's Resource Book*, ed. Christina Murphy and Bryon Stay, 237–45. Mahwah, NJ: Erlbaum.

Healy, Dave. 1995. "Writing Center Directors: An Emerging Portrait of the Profession." *Writing Program Administration* 18 (3): 26–43.

Hobson, Eric. 1994. "Writing Center Theory Counters Practice: So What?" In *Intersections: Theory/Practice in the Writing Center*, ed. Joan Mullin and Ray Wallace, 1–10. Urbana, IL: National Council of Teachers of English.

Holbrook, Sue Ellen. 1991. "Women's Work: The Feminizing of Composition." *Rhetoric Review* 9 (2): 201–29. http://dx.doi.org/10.1080/07350199109388929.

hooks, bell. 1994. *Teaching to Transgress*. New York: Routledge.

Hult, Christina, David Joliffe, Kathleen Kelly, Dana Meade, and Charles Schulster. 1992. "The Portland Resolution: Guidelines for Writing Program Administrator Positions." *WPA: Writing Program Administration* 16 (1/2): 88–94.

Ianetta, Melissa, Linda Bergman, Lauren Fitzgerald, Carol Peterson Haviland, Lisa Lebduska, and Mary Wislocki. 2006. "Polylog: Are Writing Center Directors Writing Program Administrators?" *Composition Studies* 34 (2): 11–42.

Inman, James. 2010. "Designing Multiliteracy Centers: A Zoning Approach." In *Multiliteracy Centers*, ed. David Sheridan and James Inman, 19–32. Cresskill, NJ: Hampton Press.

Isaacs, Emily. 2011. "The Emergence of Centers for Writing Excellence." In *Before and After the Tutorial*, ed. Nicholas Mauriello, William Macauley, and Robert Koch, 131–50. Cresskill, NJ: Hampton.

Jackson, Rebecca. 2008. "Resisting Institutional Narratives: One Student's Counterstories of Writing and Learning in the Academy." *Writing Center Journal* 28 (1): 23–42.

Jackson, Rebecca, and Jackie Grutsch McKinney. 2011. "Beyond Tutoring: Mapping the Invisible Landscape of Writing Center Work." *Praxis: A Writing Center Journal* 9 (1): np.

Jarratt, Susan C. 2003. "Feminism and Composition: The Case for Conflict." In *Feminism and Composition: A Critical Sourcebook*, ed. Gesa Kirsch, Faye Spencer Maor, Lance Massey, Lee Nickoson-Massey, and Mary P. Sheridan-Rabideau, 263–80. Boston: Bedford/St. Martin's.

Johnson-Shull, Lisa, and Diane Kelly-Riley. 2001. "Writes of Passage: Conceptualizing the Relationship of Writing Center and Writing Assessment Practices." In *Beyond Outcomes: Assessment and Instruction within a University Writing Program*, ed. Richard Haswell, 83–92. Westport, CT: Ablex.

Kiedaisch, Jean, and Sue Dinitz. 2007. "Changing Notions of Difference in the Writing Center: The Possibilities of Universal Design." *Writing Center Journal* 27 (2): 39–59.

Kingery, David, ed. 1996. *Learning from Things: Method and Theory of Material Culture Studies.* Washington, DC: Smithsonian Institution Press.

Kinkead, Jeanette. 1996. "National Writing Center Association as Mooring: A Personal History of the First Decade." *Writing Center Journal* 16 (2): 131–43.

Kinkead, Joyce, and Jeanette Harris, eds. 1993. *Writing Centers in Context: Twelve Case Studies.* Urbana, IL: National Council of Teachers of English.

Kirsch, Gesa, and Joy Ritchie. 1995. "Beyond the Personal: Theorizing a Politics of Location in Composition Research." *College Composition and Communication* 46: 7–29.

Koch, Robert. 2011. "Centers for Writing Excellence and the Construction of Civic Relationships." In *Before and After the Tutorial,* ed. Nicholas Mauriello, William Macauley, and Robert Koch, 151–64. Cresskill, NJ: Hampton.

Lakoff, George. 2005. *Don't Think of an Elephant.* River Junction, VT: Chelsea Green.

Lerner, Neal. 2000. "Confessions of a First-Time Writing Center Director." *Writing Center Journal* 21 (2): 29–48.

Lerner, Neal. 2007. "Rejecting the Remedial Brand: The Rise and Fall of the Dartmouth Writing Clinic." *College Composition and Communication* 59 (1): 13–35.

Lerner, Neal. 2009. *The Idea of a Writing Laboratory.* Carbondale: Southern Illinois University Press.

Lerner, Neal, and Paula Gillespie. 2003. *The Allyn and Bacon Guide to Peer Tutoring.* 2nd ed. New York: Longman.

Lotto, Edward. 1993. "The Lehigh University Writing Center: Creating a Community of Writers." In *Writing Centers in Context,* ed. Joyce Kinkead and Jeanette Harris, 78–96. Urbana, IL: National Council of Teachers of English.

Lunsford, Andrea. 2001. "Collaboration, Control, and the Idea of a Writing Center." In *The Allyn and Bacon Guide to Writing Center Theory and Practice,* ed. Robert Barnett and Jacob Blumner, 92–99. Boston: Allyn and Bacon.

Lunsford, Andrea. 2008. Keynote Address at the East Central Writing Center Association Conference. Columbus, OH.

Lyotard, Francois. 1984. *The Postmodern Condition: A Report on Knowledge.* Trans. Geoff Bennington and Brian Mussami. Minneapolis: University of Minnesota Press. http://dx.doi.org/10.2307/1772278.

Macauley, William, and Nicholas Mauriello, eds. 2007a. *Marginal Words, Marginal Works: Tutoring the Academy in the Work of Writing Centers.* Cresskill, NJ: Hampton Press.

Macauley, William, and Nicholas Mauriello. 2007b. "An Invitation to the 'Ongoing Conversation.'" In *Marginal Words, Marginal Works: Tutoring the Academy in the Work of Writing Centers,* ed. William Macauley and Nicholas Mauriello, xiii–xvi. Cresskill, NJ: Hampton Press.

Marshall, Margaret. 2001. "Sites for (Invisible) Intellectual Work." In *The Politics of Writing Centers,* ed. Jane Nelson and Kathy Evertz, 74–84. Portsmouth, NH: Boynton/Cook.

Mauriello, Nicholas, William Macauley, and Robert Koch, eds. 2011. *Before and After the Tutorial.* Cresskill, NJ: Hampton Press.

Mendelsohn, Sue. 2011. "'If You Build It, They Might Come': Constructing Writing Center Satellites." In *Before and After the Tutorial,* ed. Nicholas Mauriello, William Macauley, and Robert Koch, 89–102. Cresskill, NJ: Hampton Press.

Miller, Susan. 2003. "The Feminization of Composition." In *Feminism and Composition: A Critical Sourcebook,* ed. Gesa Kirsch, Faye Spencer Maor, Lance Massey, Lee Nickoson-Massey, and Mary P. Sheridan-Rabideau, 520–33. Boston: Bedford/St. Martins.

Mohr, Ellen. 1993. "Establishing a Writing Center for the Community." In *Writing Centers in Context,* ed. Joyce Kinkead and Jeanette Harris, 145–64. Urbana, IL: National Council of Teachers of English.

Moore, Robert H. 1950. "The Writing Clinic and the Writing Laboratory." *College English* 11 (7): 388–93. http://dx.doi.org/10.2307/586024.

Munday, Nicole Kraemer. 2011. "Writing Centers and Living Learning Communities." In *Before and After the Tutorial*, ed. Nicholas Mauriello, William J. Macauley, and Robert T. Koch, 103–118. New York: Hampton Press.

Murphy, Christina, and Joe Law, eds. 1995. *Landmark Essays on Writing Centers*. Davis, CA: Hermagoras Press.

Murphy, Christina, and Steve Sherwood, eds. 2007. *The St. Martin's Sourcebook for Writing Tutors*. 3rd ed. Boston: Bedford/St. Martin's.

Murphy, Christina, and Lory Hawkes. 2010. "The Future of Multiliteracy Centers in the E-World." In *Multiliteracy Centers*, ed. David Sheridan and James Inman, 173–188. Cresskill, NJ: Hampton.

Murphy, Christina, and Byron Stay. 2006. *The Writing Center Director's Resource Book*. Mahwah, NJ: Erlbaum.

Murray, Patricia, and Linda Bannister. 1985. "Status and Responsibilities of Writing Lab Directors: A Survey." *Writing Lab Newsletter* 9 (6): 10–1.

National Survey of Student Engagement (NSSE). 2008. *Promoting Engagement for All Students: The Imperative to Look Within*. Bloomington: Indiana University Center for Postsecondary Research.

Nelson, Maria Wilson. 1991. *At the Point of Need*. Portsmouth, NH: Boynton/Cook.

Nelson, Jane, and Margaret Garner. 2011. "Horizontal Structures for Learning." In *Before and After the Tutorial*, ed. Nicholas Mauriello, William J. Macauley, and Robert T. Koch, 7–28. New York: Hampton Press.

Nicolas, Melissa. 2004. "Where the Women Are: Writing Centers and the Academic Hierarchy." *Writing Lab Newsletter* 29 (1): 11–3.

Nicolas, Melissa. 2007. "Why There Is No Happily Ever After." In *Marginal Words, Marginal Works: Tutoring the Academy in the Work of Writing Centers*, ed. William Macauley and Nicholas Mauriello, 1–18. New York: Hampton Press.

North, Stephen M. 1984. "The Idea of a Writing Center." *College English* 46 (5): 433–46. http://dx.doi.org/10.2307/377047.

North, Stephen M. 1987. *The Making of Knowledge in Composition*. Portsmouth, NH: Boynton/Cook.

North, Stephen, and Lil Brannon. 2000. "The Uses of the Margins." *Writing Center Journal* 20 (2): 7–12.

O'Hear, Michael F. 1983. "Homemade Instructional Videotapes: Easy, Fun, and Effective." *Writing Lab Newsletter* 7 (6): 1–4.

Olson, Gary A. 1984. *Writing Centers: Theory and Administration*. Urbana, IL: National Council of Teachers of English.

Olson, Gary A., and Jean-Francois Lyotard. 1995. "Resisting a Discourse of Mastery." *JAC* 15 (3): 391–410.

Pemberton, Michael. 2011. "Revisiting 'Tales Too Terrible to Tell': A Survey of Graduate Coursework in Writing Program and Writing Center Administration." In *Before and After the Tutorial*, ed. Nicholas Mauriello, William J. Macauley, and Robert T. Koch, 255–74. New York: Hampton Press.

Penner, Catherine. 1998. "Narrative Theory." In *Theorizing Composition*, ed. Mary Lynch Kennedy, 195–99. Westport, CT: Greenwood Press.

Perdue, Virginia, and Deborah James. 1990. "Teaching in the Center." *Writing Lab Newsletter* 14 (10): 7–8.

Primary Research Group. 2009. "Survey of American College Students: Use of and Satisfaction with College Tutoring Services." Primary Research Group, Inc. http://www.primaryresearch.com/view_product.php?report_id=163.

Porter, James. 1986. "Intertextuality and the Discourse Community." *Rhetoric Review* 5 (1): 34–47. http://dx.doi.org/10.1080/07350198609359131.

"The Portland Resolution." 1992. *WPA: Writing Program Administration* 16 (1–2): 88–94.

Rafoth, Ben, ed. 2000. *A Tutor's Guide.* Portsmouth, NH: Boynton/Cook.

Reynolds, Nedra. 1998. "Composition's Imagined Geographies: The Politics of Space in the Frontier, City, and Cyberspace." *College Composition and Communication* 50 (1): 12–35. http://dx.doi.org/10.2307/358350.

Rihn, Andrew. 2010. "Resistance One-on-One." *Journal of Marxism and Interdisciplinary Inquiry* 3 (2): 20–4.

Riley, Terrance. 1994. "The Unpromising Future of Writing Centers." *Writing Center Journal* 15 (1): 20–34.

Robertson, Linda, Sharon Crowley, and Frank Lentricchia. 1987. "The Wyoming Conference Resolution Opposing Unfair Salaries and Working Conditions for Post-Secondary Teachers of Writing." *College English* 49 (3): 274–80. http://dx.doi.org/10.2307/377922.

Royster, Jacqueline Jones, and Jean C. Williams. 1999. "History in the Spaces Left: African American Presence and Narratives of Composition Studies." *College Composition and Communication* 50 (4): 563–84. http://dx.doi.org/10.2307/358481.

Rushdie, Salman. 2000. *Shame.* New York: Picador.

Ryan, Leigh, and Lisa Zimmerelli. 2009. *The Bedford Guide for Writing Tutors.* 5th ed. Boston: Bedford/St. Martin's.

Sanford, Daniel. 2012. "The Peer-Interactive Writing Center at the University of New Mexico." *Composition Forum* 25: np.

Shaughnessy, Mina. 1977. *Errors and Expectations: A Guide for the Teacher of Basic Writing.* New York: Oxford University Press.

Sheridan, David, and James Inman, eds. 2010. *Multiliteracy Centers: Writing Center Work, New Media, and Multimodal Rhetoric.* Cresskill, NJ: Hampton.

Simpson, Jeanne. 1995a. "Perceptions, Realities, and Possibilities." In *Writing Center Perspectives,* ed. Byron Stay, Christina Murphy, and Eric Hobson, 48–52. Emmitsburg, MD: NWCA Press.

Simpson, Jeanne. 1995b. "What Lies Ahead for Writing Centers: Position Statement on Professional Concerns." In *Landmark Essays on Writing Centers,* ed. Christina Murphy and Joe Law, 57–62. Davis, CA: Hermagoras Press.

Simpson, Jeanne, Steve Braye, and Beth Boquet. 1994. "War, Peace, and Writing Center Administration." *Composition Studies* 22 (1): 65–95.

Simon, Linda. 1993. "The Writing Center at Harvard University." In *Writing Centers in Context,* ed. Joyce Kinkead and Jeanette Harris, 114–126. Urbana, IL: National Council of Teachers of English.

Smith, Louise Z. 2003. "Independence and Collaboration: Why We Should Decentralize Writing Centers." *Writing Center Journal* 23 (2): 15–23.

Soven, Margot Iris. 2006. *What the Writing Tutor Needs to Know.* Boston: Wadsworth.

Spigelman, Candace, and Laurie Grobman. 2005. *On Location.* Logan: Utah State University Press.

Steele, Mildred. 2002. "Professional Status for Writing Center Directors." In *Histories of Developmental Education,* ed. Dana Britt Lundell and Jeanne Higbee, 59–63. St. Paul: University of Minnesota Center for Research on Developmental Education and Urban Literacy.

Trimmer, Joseph, ed. 1997. *Narration as Knowledge.* Portsmouth, NH: Heinemann.

Valentine, Kathryn. 2008. "The Potential and Perils of Expanding the Space of the Writing Center." *Writing Center Journal* 28 (1): 63–78.

Vescio, Don. 1998. "Website Design for a Writing Center." *Writing Lab Newsletter* 23 (2): 7–9.

Weaver, Marilyn. 2006. "A Call for Racial Diversity in the Writing Center." In *Writing Center Director Resource Book,* ed. Christina Murphy and Byron Stay, 79–92. Mahwah, NJ: Erlbaum.

Wenger, Etienne. 1999. *Communities of Practice: Learning, Meaning, and Identity.* Cambridge: Cambridge University Press.

White, Hayden. 1987. *The Content of the Form: Narrative Discourse and Historical Representation.* Baltimore: Johns Hopkins University Press.

Writing Center Research Project. "Survey Data Reports 2001–02, 2003–04, 2005–06, and 2007–08." Accessed December 6, 2012. http://coldfusion.louisville.edu/webs/a-s/wcrp/reports/index.cfm.

Yergeau, Melanie, Kathryn Wozniak, and Peter Vandenberg. 2008. "Expanding the Space of f2f: Writing Centers and Audio-Visual-Textual Conferencing." *Kairos* 13 (1): np.

INDEX

ABOUT THE AUTHOR

JACKIE GRUTSCH MCKINNEY is associate professor of rhetoric and composition at Ball State University. She has published articles in several edited collections, *The Writing Center Journal, Writing Lab Newsletter, Praxis,* and *WPA: The Journal of the Council of Writing Program Administrators.* She is currently working on a collaborative case study project of new writing center directors.

Made in the USA
Lexington, KY
21 January 2018